A

SUSSEX F

A SUSSEX FAMILY

*The family of Ridge from 1500
to the present day*

by

Dudley Ridge

Phillimore

1975

Published by

PHILLIMORE & CO. LTD.
London and Chichester

Head Office: Shopwyke Hall,
Chichester, Sussex, England.

© Dudley Ridge, 1975

ISBN O 85033 076 9

Printed by Unwin Brothers Limited
at The Gresham Press
Old Woking, Surrey, England

'The family of the Ridges is ancient; as early as the commencement of Queen Elizabeth's reign they inherited property in Iford; and it has descended through numerous generations, uninterrupted, to the present possessor.'

T.W. Horsfield, *The History and Antiquities of Lewes and its Vicinity* (1827).

CONTENTS

I	Pedigree	1
II	The Yeoman Farmer	4
III	The Two Johns	11
IV	Interlude — The Domestic Scene	16
V	The Three Stephens	21
VI	The First Gentleman	28
VII	The Man of Purpose	40
VIII	'The Old Order Changeth'	50
IX	The Individualists	55
	Epilogue	60
	References	62
	Bibliography	63
	Appendix	
	Wills	65
	Post Mortem Inventories	75
	Deed of Conveyance, Woodbrookes	82
	Armorial Bearings of Ridge Family	84
	Pedigree — Direct Descent	86
	Pedigree — Iford Branch	88
	Index	89

LIST OF PLATES

(Between pp. 36 and 37)

1	The Ridge Country
2	Burnt House Farm, Fletching
3	Ovingdean Church
4	Iford Church
5	Tudor Farmhouse, Iford
6	Woodbrookes Farm, Chailey
7	Upper Stoneham, South Malling
8	Tulley Wells, Hamsey
9	Alciston Place
10	Alciston Place, Tithe Barn
11	Ridge and Johnson Vaults, Lewes
12	St. Anne's House, Lewes
13	Lewes Town Book
14	'We the Undersigned'

LIST OF FIGURES

1	The Ridge Country	3
2	Part of Iford Tithe Map, 1840	6
3	Journey into Kent, 1744	34

PREFACE

In *We the Undersigned*, a history of the Royal London Mutual Insurance Society, Ltd., the late W. Gore Allen described the co-founder, Henry Ridge, as a man 'with his roots deep in the soil of the south country.' Although Henry was born in London, he was of Sussex stock descended from a Tudor farmer and an 18th-century diarist.

At the suggestion of Mr. E.H. Haynes, Chairman of the Royal London, the author undertook the task of searching for information which would throw some light on the ancestors of Henry Ridge.

During the past four years a large amount of interesting material has been collected and the most difficult task has been the selection of those portions most suitable for the production of this book.

Valuable evidence has been obtained from Wills and Post Mortem Inventories at the East Sussex Records Office, Lewes, and from collections of deeds in the Muniment Room of the Sussex Archaeological Society.

The author is particularly indebted to the Directors of the Royal London for their continued interest, encouragement and generous assistance with costs of publication; to Mr. Alan D. Ridge, Provincial Archivist, Alberta, Canada; Dr. Jessie Ridge of Alfriston; Mr. H.C. Robinson of Iford; Mr. A.J. Roper of Kingston near Lewes; Lt. Colonel J.R.B. Walker of The College of Arms; Mr. A.J. Camp of the Society of Genealogists; Mr. N.E.S. Norris of Sussex Archaeological Society; Mr. P.R. Morris, Town Clerk of Lewes; Mr. L.S. Davey of Lewes and to many others who have contributed so willingly to the search for evidence.

Finally, this work would never have been completed without the co-operation and encouragement of Mrs. Winifred Violet Ridge who has spent many hours searching and transcribing documents and while (like most wives) gracefully accepting her husband's family, has had to bear with eleven generations of ancestors as well!

DUDLEY RIDGE

CHAPTER I

PEDIGREE

THE REV. T.W. HORSFIELD in his *History and Antiquities of Lewes* (1827) gives several family trees of the Ridge family, one of which terminates with the children of Richard Ridge of Fletching. The youngest of these was George Henry, the father of Henry Ridge and the author's great-grandfather. It is thus possible to construct a pedigree for the Ridge family starting from a John Ridge of Ovingdean right down to the present generation. Such a family tree, whilst showing dates of births, deaths and marriages, tells us nothing of the people themselves. It is like a railway timetable showing all the stations between London and Edinburgh with times of arrival and departure but completely devoid of any information about the towns themselves and the countryside in which they are situated. In this book the author has endeavoured to change a list of names into real people and to give some idea of their background and the times in which they lived.

In order to construct a valid pedigree, continuity between successive generations must be shown and supported by documentary evidence. In 1537 Henry VIII ordered the compulsory keeping of Parish Registers in which were recorded the baptisms, deaths, and sometimes the marriages of the parishioners. Some years elapsed before these registers were in general use but they can usually furnish useful information from about 1560 until the Central Registry at Somerset House was started in 1837. It is therefore possible in many cases to trace a family pedigree back to the time of Elizabeth I but beyond that there are great difficulties unless the family is a noble one, when copies of Patents of Enoblement, documents relating to grants of land and manorial rolls will have been preserved. Even then, it is an ancient family that traces its line back to the 14th century and the five that claim descent from the time of the Norman Conquest give rise to controversy among genealogists.

The name of Ridge in its Old English form, *Hricge,* is found in Anglo-Saxon Charters of the 8th century, although in this context it is a place name rather than a patronymic. On his return from the Crusades in 1274, Edward I appointed circuit commissioners to enquire into alleged abuses of power by sheriffs and their subordinates. In their report (the Hundred Roll for Sussex) the commissioners note that 'John de Bretagne has warrant wherever he has land in the Rape of Hastings, and gallows and the assize of bread and ale. Adam Ridge (de Regge) and other bailiffs of the said John de Bretagne take yearly . . . by extortion 5½ marks beyond the money which used to be given in the time of Countess Alice of Eu.' In the Hundred of Baldslow it is reported that 'Thomas Ridge and Richard of Baldslow came at harvest time in the name of Matthew of Hastings, then Sheriff, and there took 6 sacks of oats worth 3s. and hay to the value of 2s. and carried them away'.

Although Adam and Thomas appear to show some of the financial acumen which characterised later members of the family, the fact that they bear the same surname does not necessarily mean that they can be claimed as ancestors. On the contrary when one considers that the majority of surnames are derived from occupations (Smith, Miller, Hunter etc.) or from topographical features (Hill, Wood, Ridge etc.), the probability is that they are not even of the same family. However satisfying it might be to include Adam and Thomas as 13th-century ancestors, there is no supporting documentary evidence and John Ridge of Ovingdean must be accepted as the first of the line.

Pedigree

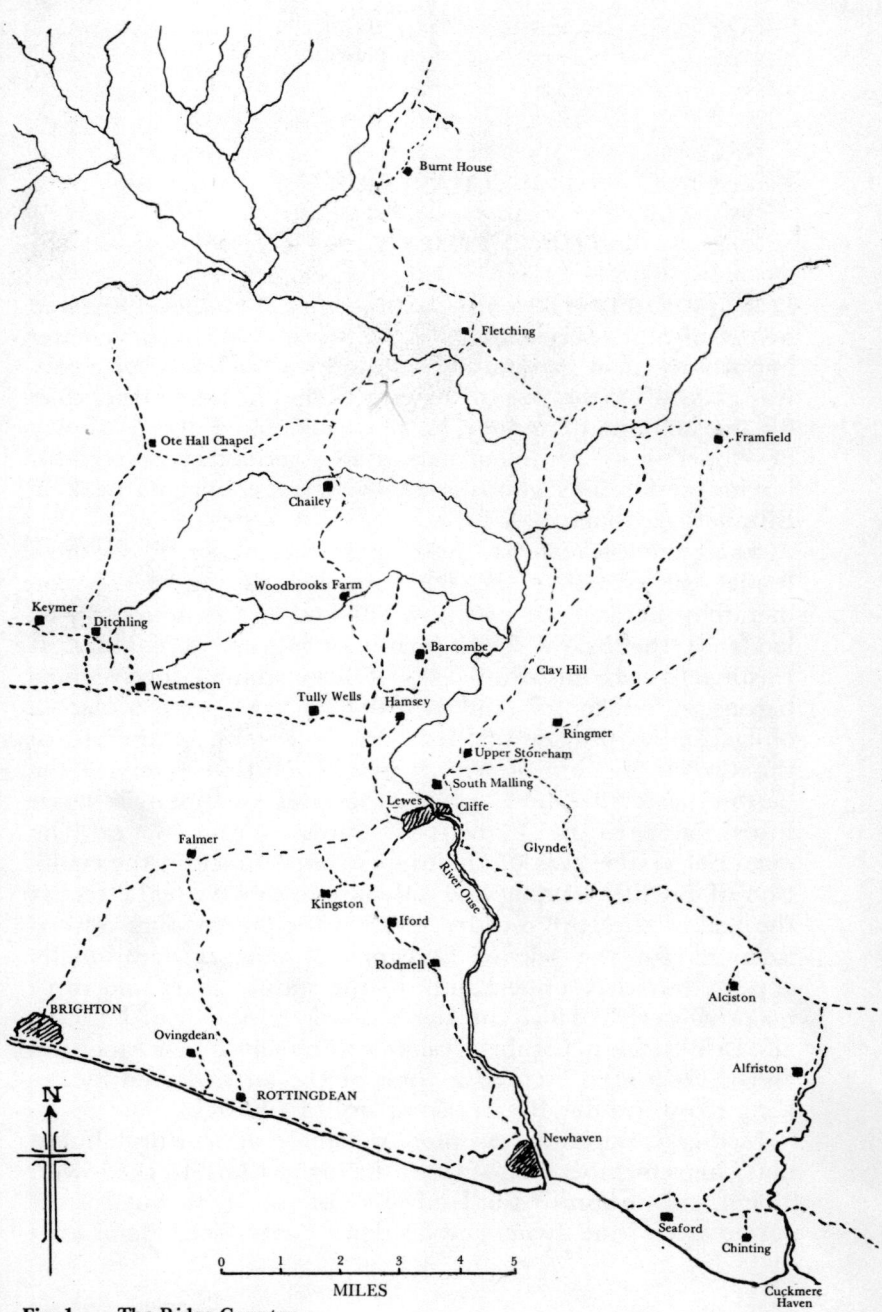

Fig. 1 The Ridge Country

CHAPTER II

THE YEOMAN FARMER

IT IS IMPORTANT to bear in mind that in medieval England ownership or occupation of lands was of much greater importance than material wealth and the 'richness' of a man was gauged by the size of the estates that he held rather than by the amount of money he possessed. As England slowly developed into a trading nation so a monetary system for buying and selling goods was evolved, reaching its peak in Elizabethan times.

The common man had fewer privileges under the Norman feudal system than he had enjoyed during the Saxon hierarchy because he was now subject to a conqueror. The lands of the Saxon lords (many of whom were killed at Hastings), were distributed by William among the Norman barons in return for 'service', that is they were under an obligation to provide and lead private armies for the use of the Crown in time of war. Again in return for service the barons bartered parcels of their estates (manors) to lesser lords, later to be known as 'Lords of the Manor'. The manorial system was of the utmost importance in the evolution of English farming and only ceased to have real effect at the end of the 19th century. Even at the present time advertisements for the sale of lordships of manors occasionally appear, but they appeal only to the status seeker and carry no privileges. In 1967 the Lordship of the Manor of Felsham and Drinkstone in Cambridgeshire was bought by an American and shortly after figured as one of the gifts offered by the King Korn Trading Stamp Company of Chicago!

Medieval England was predominantly agricultural but it must be remembered that from the highest lord to the lowest villein, cultivation of the land was not for profit but for the sustenance of the owner and his dependants. The villeins lived in villages on the manor and had a strip of land to farm in the open field together with grazing rights on the common land. They were completely at the disposal of the lord of the manor and could not marry or move away from their village without his consent. Furthermore for certain days in each year the villein was obliged to work on the lord's desmesne, particularly at harvest time, with the result that crops in the open field were often spoilt and the village went hungry. The map of the Iford farmlands in 1840 (Plate 2) shows how the divisions of the Open Field had persisted for 400 years and, in fact, the name remained in use as long as the manor existed. An entry[1] on the Court Roll of the Manor of Northease-cum-Iford in 1850 contains the phrase 'All that messuage tenement barn and customary land lying in the Common Fields of Iford . . .'.

Even more striking is the photograph of a wheat field at Firle (Plate 1). Here the Common Fields have long been merged into one, the ground ploughed, sown and harvested year after year, yet in the oblique rays of the setting sun the old divisions are clearly visible.

Over the years it became apparent that the feudal system had certain drawbacks in that the tillage of the lord's desmesne by half-starved labourers, often suffering from nutritional diseases, was not the most efficient way of farming. It gradually became the practice for the more competent husbandmen to be allowed to cultivate parts of the manor estate in return for which an agreed portion of the produce was given to the lord. Other estate owners found that it was more profitable to employ labourers all the year round rather than to depend on the feudal 'work days'. The increase in population in the 13th century caused a recession in commutation of service and the agents of the lords were able to force on the starving population a return to 'work days' in exchange for farming concessions. On the other hand, the Black Death which halved the population of England in 1348-49, so reduced the available labour force that not only were work days commuted for monetary payments or tenure of land but the lords of the manor were obliged to grant long leases of the manorial desmesne to a new class of freemen known as 'franklins' and later as 'yeomen'. The only excep-

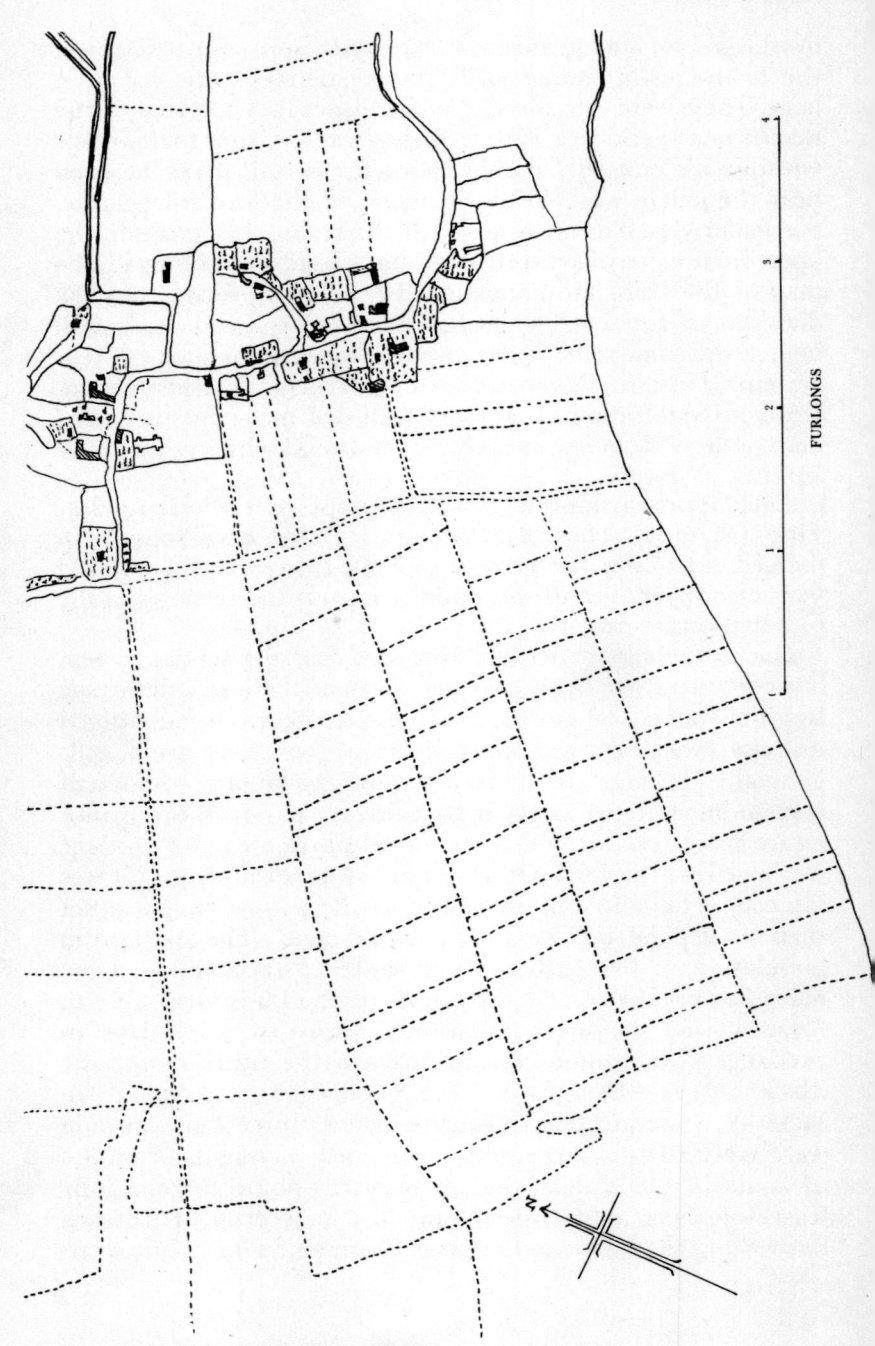

Fig. 2 Part of Iford Tithe Map, 1840

The Yeoman Farmer

tions were the great religious houses such as St. Edmundsbury where the abbots continued to exact their feudal rights in full and against whom was directed the fury of the Peasants' Revolt in 1381.

No specific date can be given for the end of the feudal system because there was no abrupt change from one system to another such as occurred during the French Revolution. Like most of the social and economic changes in the life of the English people, the process was evolutionary. Towards the close of the 15th century strip farming in the open field was still prevalent, but serfdom had practically disappeared. By the time Elizabeth I was on the throne, England was firmly established as a commercial nation and money was of importance not only to the merchants of the big towns but also to those engaged in agriculture. The yeoman farmer had been born, owning his own land, socially intermediate between the husbandman and the gentleman and differing only from the latter in that he worked with his hands.

Although the feudal system had completely disappeared by the end of the 16th century, the focal point of farming in Elizabethan and Jacobean times was still the Manor. The Lord of the Manor held his lands of the overlord by purchase instead of by service and the tenants of the manor paid rentals instead of holding their land by 'work days'. The steward of the manor held a Manor Court or Court Leet at regular intervals to settle disputes and to record changes of tenancy and these courts persisted, with modifications, until the 20th century. Procedure was determined by custom as set out in the 'Custumal of the Manor' which preserved a number of manorial rights dating from feudal times, albeit modified in the process of time.

In tracing the development of the Ridge family we are concerned with manors in the vicinity of Lewes which came under the Barony of Lewes originally held by Earl de Warenne, son-in-law of William the Conqueror. By the end of the 16th century the Barony had become divided but the major portion was held by Lord Bergavenny (Abergavenny). John Rowe, a lawyer of some eminence, held the office of Steward from 1597 to 1622 and during this time made a detailed survey[2] of all the manors in the Barony together with their respective Custumals. He recorded the lands held by each tenant, the nature of the tenancy and the rents and fines (fees) due to the Lord.

'Copyhold tenants' were the descendants of those who in earlier days had been obliged to perform customary work on the lord's desmesne. These tenants had no lease or documentary evidence of title but held their land by 'Copy of Court Roll'. Although traditionally they were tenants 'at the will of the lord' and owed him 'fealty', copyholders by Rowe's time had evolved into rent-paying tenants and could dispose of their holding by will or by alienation, subject to certain conditions of custom. On the death of a tenant copyhold land was 'surrendered to the use of his will' and the inheritor had to attend the Manor Court to be placed on the Roll, paying the prescribed dues or fines.

In feudal days the lord had the right of 'heriot', that is he was entitled to take the best beast of the deceased tenant. By the 16th century fealty to the lord and the right of heriot had been commuted to payments in cash but the procedure remained unaltered until a series of Acts of Parliament beginning in 1852 and culminating in the Law of Property Act (1925), eventually granted complete enfranchisement of copyhold land. The strict adherence to custom (dating from feudal times) is shown in a copy of the Court Roll for the Manor of Northease-cum-Iford dated 1850.[3]

'Whereas William Ridge late of Stoneham . . . Gentleman held of the Lord of the said Manor . . . by Copy of Court Roll at the Will of the Lord according to the Custom of the Manor all that messuage . . . and two yards of customary land lying in the Common Fields of Iford paying to the Lord yearly twenty shillings . . . sometime since died seized thereof upon which happened to the Lord for Heriots three Oxen which were seized and have been compounded for at Twenty Four Pounds . . . By his last Will and Testament . . . gave all his Real Estate to his only brother Henry Ridge . . . to whom the Lord of the said Manor by the said Steward grants Seizin thereof by the Rod . . . by Copy of Court Roll . . . he is admitted Tenant thereof . . . pays to the said Lord for Fines one hundred and eight pounds and his Fealty is respited.'

The Book of John Rowe furnishes much interesting information about the customs associated with the tenure of copyhold land. Rents in the early part of the 17th century were generally low and in the Manor of Northease-cum-Iford maximum rents for arable land and marsh (i.e. grazing) were 1s. and 2s. per acre respectively. Rowe quotes examples of the old feudal 'payment in kind', all of which by his time had, of course, been commuted to monetary payments. 'One penny or one arrow; twopence or two brode arrow heads; a race of ginger; half a barell of herrings'. The last was a fine for inscribing a change of ownership on the Court Roll. All the manors in the Barony of Lewes followed the custom of 'Borough English' by which the youngest son inherited ('at the will of the Lord') on the death of a copyholder. The widow, however, could exercise the right of 'Widow's Bench' by which she retained possession of her deceased husband's copyhold lands until her own death. The lands would eventually revert to the youngest son who probably worked the farm during the lifetime of his mother.

Originally a husbandman was anyone who cultivated the land, but with the evolution of the freeholder, the name in Elizabethan times had become restricted to those who were copyholders, whilst those who held free land to the value of 40s. per annum were classed as yeomen.[4] This 'free land' might be such that the yeoman had absolute title to it (freehold in the modern sense), but the usual practice was for the over-lord to grant a long lease, thus retaining the ownership for his heirs, whilst the yeoman on his part was free to use the land as he wished and in addition to sell the lease without the manorial procedure implicit in copyhold transactions. Among the Iford Farm Deeds is a note of a lease for 1,000 years of a 'Barn and two Yardlands' granted by Mr. Thomas Ade to Mr. William Ridge in 1729 to 'serve the payment of 400 lb with interest'.

The Dissolution of the Monasteries (1537-39), had brought many thousands of acres into the hands of the big landowners and by the end of the 16th century much of this land was being re-sold in small lots. Dr. Campbell,[5] has shown that between 1570 and 1640, 37 per cent. of yeoman land purchases were for sums less than £50, whilst only eight per cent. cost more than £500. Even allowing for the greater purchasing power of Elizabethan money, the land prices were not exorbitant, ranging from 9d. for a single rood to £2,100 for a sizeable estate.

CHAPTER III

THE TWO JOHNS

JOHN RIDGE OF OVINGDEAN
Husbandman. 1506?-1558

OVINGDEAN is a small village lying a mile or so inland from the coast between Brighton and Rottingdean. Somewhere in the churchyard of the ancient church of St. Wulfran lies the body of John Ridge, the first recorded ancestor of the Ridge family. The parish registers tell us nothing about him as they only date from 1705, but fortunately the wills (see appendix, p.64-66) of both John and his wife, Agnes, have survived and it is from these documents that most of the information about this Tudor farmer has been obtained.

John Ridge had married Agnes Pollington who was probably a local girl since Richard Pollington (her brother?) witnessed her will and was a legatee in that of her husband. When John died in 1558 they had four children, two sons, John and Thomas and two daughters, Agnes and Tompson. John was the eldest, over 21 years of age since he was co-executor of his father's will and presumably unmarried as there is no mention of a wife in either testament. As the average age of Tudor bridegrooms was 28,[6] he would be about 25 years old. The daughter Agnes was probably the second child as she bears her mother's christian name and although single at the time of her father's death was married and living in Hampshire a year later. Tompson, the second daughter was unmarried and Thomas was still a minor when his mother died.

In the mother's will there are bequests to all the children by name and then the rather curious legacy, 'Item I geve to my sonne Bottyng and to my dowghter his wyfe £iiij of lawfull monye of England Item I wyll that my dowghter Bottyng shall have my best kerchief'. At first sight this suggests that there was a third daughter but only two daughters are mentioned in John's will and in that of his wife, Agnes is referred to as 'my dowghter in Hamshere', leading to the conclusion that Agnes had married a Bottyng and moved into the next county.

Assuming that John the eldest son was 25 and that his father married at the age of 26, John of Ovingdean would have been born in the last years of the reign of Henry VII and would have been a year or two over 50 when he died. Although this deduction is in accordance with the expectancy of life at that period[7] it is not conclusive, particularly as succeeding generations showed remarkable longevity.

Although only holding lands at the will of the Lord of the Manor of Withdean Cayliffe, John of Ovingdean appears from his will to have been quite a prosperous farmer owning cattle, sheep and arable land. Furthermore he was able to bequeath £10 to each of his unmarried children and the total value of his estate was estimated at £95 6s. 11d. — a large sum for those days.

Gregory King, who in 1688 made a survey of family incomes,[8] gave £44 as the average annual income of a husbandman with four children and 100 years earlier the amount would have been considerably smaller.

John of Ovingdean lived through the tumultuous reign of Henry VIII, the six short years of the boy king, Edward VI and as Queen Mary outlived him by one week he died, as he was born, a Catholic. Elizabeth I had been on the throne nearly a year when Agnes Ridge was laid beside her husband in Ovingdean churchyard. She died a Protestant but was probably quite unaware of it.

The location of the Ridge farm in Ovingdean is not known but it could have been on the hills to the north-east of the village where the Manor of Withdean Cayliffe marched with the Manor of Northease-cum-Iford into which the eldest son of John of Ovingdean moved not long after the death of his mother. There is a farm called Norton in this area and it may be significant that at a later date the Ridges held 71 acres of grazing land on Norton Down.

JOHN RIDGE OF IFORD
Yeoman. 1533?-1612

WHEN AGNES RIDGE DIED in 1559 the farmlands would pass to her youngest son, Thomas, according to the custom of Borough English. At about the same time John, the eldest son was married and moved to Iford on the west bank of the River Ouse, a few miles downstream from Lewes. All that is known about his wife is that her name was Joane and that she was buried at Iford on 2 November 1609.

John's transfer to Iford moved him up in the social scale for at some time or other he became possessed of 'free' land and was the first yeoman in the family. The property may have been acquired by purchase, by marrying a wife with land as a dowry or it may have been given as a reward for service (see p.21). There is little doubt that in his later years he was rich enough to add to his estates by purchase and probably because he had become a man of some importance he styled himself 'A'Ridge'. This soon became 'Aridge' which remained the family name for some 70 years until John's grandson reverted to the original patronymic.

Whilst there is no evidence to show how or when free land was acquired, consideration of the origin of the Iford estate is based on firmer grounds. When the great religious houses were dissolved in 1539, all their revenues were assigned to the king. He in turn granted lands (for a cash consideration) to those who had been of assistance to him in this particular form of banditry. Now the Cluniac Priory of St. Pancras at Lewes although exceedingly wealthy held no lands in chief, due no doubt to the rather unusual circumstances of its foundation. For his services to William the Conqueror in the invasion of England, William de Warenne (married to the King's daughter, Gundrada) was given many large estates including the Rape of Lewes, one sixth of the whole county of Sussex. In 1070 de Warenne installed four monks from Cluny at Southover to form the nucleus of the Priory of St.

Pancras. Grants of land were made from the de Warenne estates[9] but the astute baron avoided outright gifts and granted long leases only. During the years this practice was followed by other benefactors and although at the Dissolution the revenues of St. Pancras were estimated at £1,091 9s. 6d.[10] (about £40,000 in present day money), the king only obtained the leases, many of which would have been bought back by the descendants of the original lessors.

Now it is probable that the free land which made John Ridge a yeoman was originally a Priory farm purchased from the assignees of Gregory Cromwell who had the property from Henry VIII. There are two pieces of evidence which support this theory. The first is in the Book of John Rowe[11] where a description of the Common Seal of the Priory is followed by '... also the date of a writing whereunto the said common seale is affixed (nowe remayninge in the custody of Stephen A'Ridge of Iforde) is ... 6 Junij 2.H.8'. The second corroboration is architectural. In Tudor days the majority of farm houses were oak-framed with the spaces between the beams filled with plaster — the so-called Elizabethan house. Fortunately the original Iford farm house is still in existence, altered through successive generations and now modernised to form two agricultural dwellings. An examination of Plate 4 clearly shows the heavy stone lintels over the lower windows and the characteristic Tudor doorway. This building, built of flints, was more substantial than the usual timber house and could be part of a Priory farm. Domesday Book records that in 1086 de Warenne held lands in Niworde (Iford) and these were subsequently leased to the Priory of St. Pancras.[12] For over 300 years the Iford lands remained in the Ridge family until on the death of Henry Ridge of Stoneham in 1871 the property passed to the female side.

John Ridge of Iford was nearly 80 years old when he died in 1612 and was undoubtedly a wealthy man. He left bequests to his children and to 11 grandchildren, legacies which enabled them in turn to maintain yeoman status.

His eldest son Stephen inherited the major portion of his estate although Richard, the second son, was sufficiently well endowed to be a yeoman and to hold the office of churchwarden. Both Stephen and Richard were Reeves[13] or officers of the manor.* The third son, George, was a yeoman farming at Rottingdean and it is interesting to note that after his death in 1598, his widow married Richard Ade whose family was closely associated with Iford and the Ridges. The only daughter, Mary, married Richard Dumbrill of Wivelsfield, but it is likely that they made their home in Iford as Richard was a customary tenant in the Manors of Southease and of Northease-cum-Iford. [14]

Most of the information about the worldly goods of John Ridge is obtained from the Post Mortem Inventory (see appendix, p.74) of which one of the overseers was his son-in-law, Richard Dumbrill. He was indeed a prosperous farmer owning 21 head of cattle, nearly 300 sheep, eight oxen, 10 hogs and two horses. Chicken, geese and ducks are not included in the Inventory, probably because they were the concern of the women of the house. He had some £40 in ready money, £104 owing to him and the whole of his personal estate was valued at £604 13s. 8d.

---

* 'There is within every Manor a Reeve who is the Lordes immediate officer. The reeve is chargeable with all the auncient quitrents of freeholders and copiholders, with the extractes of the Courts delivered to him by the Steward and with the seizinge of heriottes.' *Book of John Rowe*, p. 84.

CHAPTER IV

INTERLUDE — THE DOMESTIC SCENE

IN MEDIEVAL TIMES the farmhouse was primarily a shelter for man and beast and consisted of a lofty hall used for both eating and sleeping.[15] Smoke from a fire in the centre of the floor escaped through openings in the roof, but towards the end of the 16th century it was becoming common practice to build the hearth against a wall with a chimney running up the outside of the house. The next development was to construct a floor half way up the hall to give a number of first floor rooms which in the early days were used for storage and only later as bedrooms. A screen or wall separated the hall from the passageway connecting the front and rear doors and on the side of the passage remote from the living room food was stored, the buttery for liquids and the pantry for dry goods. The rear door opened on to the yards round which were cowsheds, pigsties, stables and a brewery. Later a kitchen was built against the outside wall of the house as a more convenient place for cooking than in the hall. The large main room was still regarded as the communal sleeping place but the head of the house and his wife usually slept in the 'parlour', formed by putting a partition across the far end of the hall. At this period earthen floors were being replaced by bricks or tiles, but were still strewn with rushes. Carpets and rugs were unsuitable for farm use and there is no mention of such luxuries in any of the post mortem inventories. Apart from painted canvas hung on the walls, the furnishings of the house were strictly utilitarian. (See Post Mortem Inventories, appendix pp.74-79). The hall or living room contained a long table, a counter (sideboard) and benches or stools, used mainly at meal times. Essential pieces of kitchen equipment were a spit for roasting, iron pots hung over the fire on hooks, an assortment of pans and wooden tubs. In the Inventory of

Interlude — The domestic scene 17

John Ridge of Iford (1710) a clock is mentioned for the first time and the austerity of pewter ware is leavened by the inclusion of a silver salt-cellar and silver spoons. Wooden and pewter platters were used in Elizabethan times but knives are not listed in inventories probably because a knife was a personal, all-purpose tool.

The house was plentifully supplied with beds, blankets, coverlets and sheets, the last no doubt reserved for use in the parlour.

The most prized of all household possessions were the chests in which were stored bed and table linen, clothes, documents and other valuables.

Also living in the farmhouse would be a ploughman, a cattleman and a woman or girl to assist the mistress, all of whom would be regarded as part of the family.[16] Wages, by our standards, were low; but entering the service of the farmer at the age of 10 a boy or girl (usually of poor family) would be housed, clothed and fed until they married and left the farm.[17] Boys and men were engaged in the heavy work especially at harvest time, whilst the women and girls kept house, prepared the meals, made dairy produce, looked after the poultry, baked bread and brewed beer. In addition they would spin and weave and use the cloth for making garments for the whole family. Every one had working clothes and a suit for holidays whilst the mistress of the house might have a more varied wardrobe. (Will of Agnes Ridge; appendix p.65).

At the beginning of the 17th century the population of England was about 6,000,000 of which three quarters was rural. With the exception of Bristol, Norwich, Southampton, York and of course, London, very few towns had more than 5,000 inhabitants. For the Iford yeoman the family was the unit and the church the centre of most communal activities. There was no communication with the outside world[18] except for the weekly journey to Lewes market and the annual visit to the town fair.

In the yeoman's family there was little time for leisure and none for frivolities.[19] Religion played an important part in the life of the whole community from the gentleman to the pauper and it was not until the Industrial Revolution had created towns with large working class populations lacking the spiritual ties of a small rural community, that church-going became a social grace of the middle class.[20] Proud of his independence and resenting interference from the government it is not surprising that the yeoman, with his simple way of life, leaned more and more towards Puritanism.

In spite of the austerity of his philosophy the yeoman lived well and never went short of food.[21] Whilst bread was the staple food, there was meat in plenty. Beef, mutton and pork eaten fresh in the summer were salted for winter consumption and there would always be bacon and ham either in the pantry or hanging from the kitchen beams. Meat pies were popular; poultry, hares and rabbits were there for the taking; and the Sussex coastal farmer could also rely on a plentiful supply of sea and river fish. Although butter and cheese were marketable goods, there was always plenty for the family. Beer, the universal drink for young and old, was brewed on the premises and as much as 200 gallons could be made for 20 shillings.[22]

From June to October everybody worked to gather in the harvest, neighbour helping neighbour. So vital was the gathering of grain for the bread that even the gentleman, who never worked with his hands, might take part without loss of status.[23] The final harvest home was celebrated with a gargantuan feast in which all, irrespective of rank, took part. After harvest came the military duties — the annual muster of all able-bodied men. This practice, originated in Tudor times, was gradually discontinued in the 17th century but the post mortem inventory of John Ridge of Iford (1612) lists his pike, corselet, tabud (tabard?) and sword.

At the close of the 16th century 60-70 per cent of the yeomen could sign their names and almost as many could read.[24] The desire to read became greater as the number of documents giving title to free land increased. The astute farmer liked to know what he had signed. During the Stuart period literacy rapidly increased and having been taught the rudiments of reading and ciphering at home, a boy showing signs of academic ability could enter a Grammar School[25] and mix with the sons of the gentry. After a good grounding in classics the scholar would proceed to one of the universities

Interlude — The domestic scene 19

or to an Inn of Court. It is of interest to note that of 13,000 students on the Register of the University of Oxford between 1567 and 1622, more than half were the sons of plebeians, that is those below the rank of gentleman.[26] More often the son of a yeoman was taught a trade especially if he were one of a large family. The boy would be properly trained in his chosen craft because the Statute of Artificers of 1563 made it illegal to engage in 'art, mystery or manuell occupation' without serving an apprenticeship.

Throughout the whole of England the early 17th century was a period of prosperity for the yeoman farmer. The previous 25 years had been an era of increasing inflation during which the price of corn had risen above that of other commodities. On the other hand the long leases held by the farmer effectively prevented any increases in the rents he had to pay on his land. There is, however, another factor which must be considered in the evaluation of the estates of Sussex and Kentish yeomen. Dr. Campbell[27] from an examination of over 2,000 yeoman wills made between 1556 and 1650, found that the average value was £160, a low figure when compared with the £600 appraisal of the goods of John of Iford (1612). In general the figures for farmers in Kent and Sussex stand well above the national average and the reason is not far to seek. From the time of Edward I, who introduced the first customs system, the inhabitants of the counties bordering the English Channel had been engaged in smuggling and by the time Elizabeth I was on the throne practically everyone, from the highest to the lowest, was involved.[28] Farmers were concerned less with 'Brandy for the parson, 'baccy for his clerk', than with the most profitable means of disposing of their wool. The export of wool to the continent was at times forbidden and at others subject to heavy duty.[29] Edward I levied half a mark (6s. 8d.) for a sack of 26 stone but with each financial crisis the charges increased and it is not surprising that large quantities of wool were shipped to the Northern Provinces from the harbours and small creeks of the Kent and Sussex coast.[30] During the reign of Mary customs rates, which had remained unchanged for over 100 years, were drastically revised, some of them being increased by as much as 75 per cent.[31] From now onwards smuggling was established as a local industry in the maritime counties and accounted for at least half of the English exports and imports.[32] 'Owling', or the illegal export of wool, was widespread in the two famous sheep-breeding counties of Kent and Sussex and all sheep owners from the gentry downwards were involved. In the initial stages the capital outlay to provide ships and equipment would have been borne by the richer landowners but so successful was owling, however, that it soon paid its own way and still showed a handsome margin of profit. It is possible that John Ridge of Iford was given some freehold land as a reward for his ability as an owler and Iford, situated on the River Ouse, was certainly a better operational centre than Ovingdean. In the middle of the 17th century, the third Stephen Ridge was installed by his father at Chailey and it is significant that Woodbrookes Farm was connected to the Ouse by a small but navigable stream. Always of importance to the Sussex farmer, owling became a major industry when in 1614 the export of wool was entirely forbidden, a ban which was not removed until 1825.[33] There can be little doubt that the increasing prosperity of the Ridge family although owing much to successive generations of good business men, was considerably augmented by the export of uncustomed wool.

However scrupulous a Sussex farmer might be in business and religion, he would never have considered owling as dishonest. He was simply maintaining his right to deal with his own possessions as he wished and at the same time resisting the iniquitous impositions of a central government which was as remote to him as the American colonies.

CHAPTER V

THE THREE STEPHENS

STEPHEN (I) RIDGE OF IFORD
Yeoman. 1560?-1638

STEPHEN RIDGE (or Aridge), a yeoman in his own right, was married and had a grown-up family when he inherited the Iford estate in 1612.

Following his father's example, he added considerably to the family property and by 1615 was the only farmer resident in Iford of sufficient wealth and importance to be elected to the office of Constable. The Steward of the Barony of Lewes however, thought it unreasonable that Stephen should be burdened with this office year after year and appointed John Vynall of Kingston to the constableship. Vynall complained to the Quarter Sessions that this constituted a breach of custom but the Justices upheld the election on the grounds that although Vynall lived at Kingston, he held certain lands in Iford and thus the custom was not broken.[34]

The Ridges now occupied a substantial proportion of the lands round Iford and it is not surprising to find that farms further afield were being acquired. When Stephen's daughter Alice married James Harman in 1625, it is probable that her father installed the newly married couple in one of his outlying farms, for on his death he bequeathed the lease of Boldee Farm, Barcombe, to his son-in-law. (See will of Stephen Ridge (1638), appendix. p.66.) The two remaining daughters Dionese and Joanna, together with their husbands, apparently predeceased their father as only their children are mentioned in his will. Two of his sons died before him, both of whom nominated their father as guardian of their infant sons. One of these, Thomas, was still a minor when Stephen died and the surviving son, Stephen (II), was particularly charged with the 'guardianship and tuition' of his young nephew. (See will of Stephen (I) Ridge (1638), appendix p.66).

With increased wealth came a rise in social status and acceptance by the local gentry. Stephen (I) appointed as an overseer to his will, 'my wellbeloved freinde John Aylwin of Lewes, gent.' and there was an association with the de la Chambres, an armigerous family with estates at Rodmell, a few miles down river from Iford. It would have been possible for Stephen Ridge to enter the ranks of the gentry, for as Harrison said in *The Description of Britain* (1577), 'In England gentility is but ancient riches',[35] and in practice one generation was sufficient. No doubt the business man in Stephen felt that the time was not yet ripe to forsake work for leisure and it was not until 1711 that we find a yeoman managing his farms from a town house in Lewes. (See will of Stephen (III) Ridge of Lewes (1711). Appendix p.68.)

The extravagances of Charles I left him perpetually short of money and as Parliament continued to tighten its grip on the royal purse strings, the King began to look for fresh sources of revenue. He revived a statute of Edward I (de Militibus, 6 Edw. I) which required all those owning land above a certain value to take up their knighthood. In 1278 this was a reasonable demand as the King relied on the knights to provide fighting men for the wars. Over the years as direct recruitment replaced private armies, the practice had become obsolete until it was given a new lease of life in 1630 when the King's commissioners were sent into the counties. There must have been many thousands of moderately rich yeomen who were faced not only with the statutory legal expenses incurred in taking up a knighthood but also with grave disturbances in their way of life. A knight, at his own expense, could be called on for jury service, to act as a Justice and even to attend the Palace of Westminster as a Member of Parliament. Charles was quite well aware that strict enforcement of the law would create intolerable hardship and as his only concern was money, the commissioners were empowered to release a man from the obligation of taking up his knighthood by 'compounding'. By one single payment he was relieved from all immediate and future expenses and could continue undisturbed on his farm. In the Rape of Lewes William Ade and Stephen Aridge, both of Iford, paid £10 each for 'Composition for Knighthood'.[36] With the exception of Danegeld, this is probably the first example in English history of what in modern times is called 'the Protection Racket'!

Succeeding members of the family had occasion to thank Stephen for his foresight, for the introduction of the Poll Tax at the Restoration in 1660 imposed an annual charge of 6d. per head on those below the rank of gentleman, whilst a knight was assessed at £20.

STEPHEN (II) RIDGE OF IFORD
Yeoman. 1590?-1664

THE FIRST STEPHEN RIDGE was nearly 80 years old when he died and was succeeded by his only surviving son who, to avoid confusion, will be referred to as Stephen (II).

About the year 1620 Stephen (II) had married Mary Howell of Chinting (Chyngton), a hamlet on the cliffs between the estuaries of the Ouse and the Cuckmere. There was one child of this marriage, Thomas, born in January 1625, his mother dying in childbirth, a not uncommon occurrence in those days. Later in the year Stephen (II) married again, although the identity of his second wife is in some doubt. The Ridge pedigree in Horsfield's *History of Lewes* gives her name as Jane Alchorne of Kingston, married 3 October 1625 and buried at Iford 12 January 1660/1. The Alchornes, however, lived at Firle, (see will of Stephen (I) Ridge, 1637/8, appendix p.66), and although it is conceivable that like the Ridges the family was spreading, there is no evidence that they held land at that time in Kingston. On the other hand the pedigree of the de la Chambre family[37] shows that Jane, daughter of John de la Chambre of Rodmell and Lewes, gent., married Thomas

Mitchell of Kingston who died in 1624. In the following year she married Stephen Ridge of Iford. Whether or not the lady was Jane de la Chambre, Jane Mitchell or Jane Alchorne, the second marriage was blessed with five sons and three daughters.

In an earlier chapter a family tree was likened to a railway timetable and by an extension of the analogy Stephen (II) can be regarded as the Clapham Junction of the family.

The wealth of the family was now well established and with legacies from grandparents and farmlands from parents, each successive generation started adult life far better off than John Ridge of Ovingdean was at his death. The available land at Iford was limited and it is not surprising, therefore, that there was at this period a movement away from the district with the ultimate formation of new branches of the family. The direct line also left Iford and formed the Chailey or Lewes branch. From now onwards there are four distinct pedigrees for the families associated with Iford, Lewes, Southover and Chichester.

Egbert, fourth son of Stephen (II) died in infancy but it will be of interest to consider the five who reached maturity, beginning with the youngest, William. He was 36 years old when, in 1674, he married Hannah Packham, daughter of the Lord of the Manor of Arches, Framfield. She died at the early age of 28 and after four years as a widower, William married Mary Carter. Her sister, Hannah, was the wife of William de la Chambre, gent., another link between the two families. William Ridge remained at Iford and the Iford branch continued through his son Benjamin. His eldest son, William, married Elizabeth Ade, removed to Rottingdean and was the founder of the Chichester branch.

Richard, the next son of Stephen (II), married Mary Packham of Framfield, sister of his brother's wife Hannah. It was, in fact, a double wedding, the two brothers marrying the two sisters on 12 May 1674. Richard apparently had no liking for farming, was apprenticed to a silversmith and as a master-man practised his craft in London. He evidently retired to Iford for both he and his wife are buried in the churchyard.

The eldest son, by Mary Howell, is described as 'Thomas

Ridge of the Cliffe, draper', and his descendants form the Southover branch. He is better known as a staunch Dissenter who suffered under the harsh laws directed against those who would not conform to the requirements of the restored Episcopal Church. During the Commonwealth the Church had been disestablished, bishops abolished and religious worship reduced to a simplicity which satisfied the rural population with a traditional resentment of State interference. When Charles II returned to the throne in 1660, the Church of England was re-established and bishops restored to their former positions. The Act of Uniformity of 1662 required all ministers to accept the episcopal authority and to use the Book of Common Prayer. Those who refused (over 2,000 of them) were ejected from their livings and forbidden to hold services. The two Conventicle Acts of 1664 and 1670 imposed severe penalties on those meeting for public worship other than in an established church and if information were laid by two informers they would be rewarded with one third of the fines imposed. On 29 May 1670, some 50 inhabitants of Lewes gathered in a lane in South Malling for a service conducted by an ejected minister, Thomas Barnard, who preached on the text, 'Redeeming the time because the days are evil', (Ephesians, v. 16), an unfortunate choice as 29 May was the King's birthday! Information was laid before the Justices and fines totalling over £30 imposed. Thomas Ridge, who had attended the conventicle with his wife and daughter, was fined 30s., but as he refused to pay, goods to the value of 50s. were distrained from his shop. 'With which I parted as willingly as with any goods I ever sold'.*

Little is known of the second son, John, except that he removed to Coombe on the River Adur and is presumed to have died at the age of 50 in 1684.

---

* Connel, *The Story of an Old Meeting House*, p.10-14. See also 'A Narrative of the late proceedings of some Justices and others pretending to put in execution the late Act against Conventicles, against severable peaceable People in and about the Town of Lewes, in Sussex, only for their being quietly met to Worship God. Printed in the Year 1670'. Reprinted in Horsfield's *History of Lewes*, Vol. I, Appendix p. xxv.

The first son of the second marriage, Stephen (III), was probably his father's right-hand man and acted as his agent in collecting rents and other dues from the many outlying farms. In 1661 his father conveyed to him and his heirs for ever the freehold of a farm in Chailey called Woodbrookes, together with other lands in the same parish, although it is doubtful whether Stephen (III) ever occupied the property himself.

The Chailey property was not a new acquisition for there was a law suit[38] in 1636 between Mr. Arthur Middleton and Stephen (I) Ridge over a disputed right-of-way through Woodbrookes. Stephen also appears to have used the revenue from this property for the maintenance and education of his grandson Thomas.[39] Some of the evidence given in this source is open to serious criticism, but the Deed of Conveyance makes it quite clear that Woodbrookes was un-encumbered in 1661. (See appendix, p.81.)

STEPHEN (III) RIDGE OF WESTMESTON
Yeoman. 1626-1714

WHEN HIS FATHER DIED in 1664, Stephen (III) was 38 years old, single and probably living on one of the Ridge farms at Westmeston, above five miles from Lewes and two miles from Ditchling, where he married Joan Marchant in 1670. He was still at Westmeston in 1672 when a licence[40] under the Act of Indulgence was granted to enable Dissenters to hold services at his house.

In his later years he moved from Westmeston to the house in St. Mary's Lane (now Station Street), Lewes, where he died in 1714 aged 88.

He had a large family, four sons and six daughters, but four of the children probably died in infancy. Three of the girls found husbands in Lewes, Mary marrying George Star an upholsterer in 1707 which suggests that by that date the family was already installed in St. Mary's Lane.

About seven years before this Stephen (III) determined the tenancy of Woodbrookes in favour of his eldest son, Stephen

(IV), whilst the second son, Richard, had the lease of Upper Stoneham Farm in the parish of South Malling just outside Lewes.

It is now quite evident that a family tradition of prosperous farming had been established and successive heads of the family were prepared to leave the estates to the son best fitted to maintain and extend them. When Thomas, the eldest son of Stephen (II) showed little promise as a successful farmer his father apprenticed him to a draper and made Stephen (III) his main heir. In like manner Stephen (III) was not too sure of his eldest son Stephen as a worthy successor and in his will left him £50 and a 99-year lease on Woodbrookes. The second son, Richard, was left all the copyhold lands in the Manor of Northease-cum-Iford and the Chailey estate on the death of his brother, with the proviso that Richard should pay to the two surviving daughters of Stephen (IV) the sum of £600.

Stephen (III) was the first member of the family to have a town house in Lewes from which he managed his estates. However, he always described himself as a yeoman and it was not until the next generation that the title 'gentleman' was used.

He left substantial sums to two married daughters, an annuity to his unmarried daughter, Elizabeth, household goods and the house together with an annuity of £30 to his widow and the rest of his personal estate to his executor, Richard.

His post mortem inventory (see appendix p.77) throws some light on the size and furnishings of his house in St. Mary's Lane and although the sum is not excessive it must be remembered that here he ranked as a private householder and not as a farmer.

When his son, Stephen of Chailey, died in 1736, he was a small farmer worth £138 5s. 0d. (see appendix p.79). His father's estimate of his ability had been correct.

CHAPTER VI

THE FIRST GENTLEMAN

BY THE MIDDLE of the 17th century the Elizabethan husbandman had developed into the prosperous yeoman farmer owning many acres of valuable farmland all within easy reach of the market town of Lewes. Wealth had accumulated but although probably richer than some of his friends among the gentry, each successive Ridge had put social advancement on one side and concentrated on improving the family property even to the extent of nominating as his heir the ablest of his sons irrespective of seniority of birth.

When Stephen Ridge of Westmeston moved into the house in St. Mary's Lane, Lewes, he qualified for the status of 'gentleman' for he no longer worked as a farmer himself. No doubt he remained actively interested in his various properties and he retained the honourable title of 'yeoman' until his death. Nevertheless he initiated a new phase in the history of the family and as each succeeding generation became wealthier, active participation in farming declined and Lewes became the focal point from which the estates were managed. Even when the head of the family accepted the title of 'gentleman', it was still customary for the sons to serve their 'apprenticeship' as yeomen until they either inherited the estates or became gentlemen in their own right.

From the 18th century onwards, more documentary evidence is available than that provided by wills and post mortem inventories, some of it from the hands of Ridges themselves.

In 1890 John Sawyer[41] published extensive extracts from 'A Book of Memorandoms kept by William Ridge' and also from a similar note-book kept by William's father, Richard Ridge of South Malling. The Rev. J.J. Connell, minister of Westgate Meeting House, Lewes, had access to these sources when he wrote *The Story of an Old Meeting House* in 1916, but since then all trace of them has disappeared. The title deeds of Westgate Meeting House, the Town Books of Lewes and the Iford Farm deeds have all been valuable in providing background information.

RICHARD RIDGE OF SOUTH MALLING
Gentleman. 1681-1755

RICHARD, the second son of Stephen (III) Ridge of Westmeston was regarded by his father as a more worthy successor than his brother Stephen and was installed at Upper Stoneham Farm in the parish of South Malling. At the age of 26 he married Ann Packham, heiress of William Packham of Framfield and the first entry in his Commonplace Book reads: 'November ye 19th: 1707 I was married to Ann Packham of franfild. December ye 25th 1708 in the forenoon at nine o'Clock God was pleased to Give my son William by her. The 15th March 1708 (1709 New Style) he was Baptised by Mr. Starr of Lewes'.

From 1662 there had been two groups of Dissenters in Lewes, one Presbyterian and the other Independent. At this time the minister of the Independents was Comfort Star,[42] the son of a Kentish doctor who in 1635 had emigrated to New England and was a benefactor of the newly founded Harvard University. Here the young man was educated and after taking his M.A. returned to England but was ejected from his living in Carlisle after the passing of the Act of Uniformity. The Rev. Edward Newton, M.A., sometime Fellow of Balliol College, Oxford, was the pastor of the Presbyterians from 1662 until he resigned at the age of 83 in 1709. Richard Ridge was the nephew of that Thomas Ridge who was brought before the magistrates for attending a Conventicle in South Malling on 29 May 1670 and Thomas Barnard who preached the 'seditious' sermon, eventually shared the Presbyterian ministry with Edward Newton until they parted company in 1700 when Barnard became the first pastor of a new Meeting House at Westgate. The Independents joined the Westgate community in 1711 but the Presbyterians remained apart until 1759.

Richard's other children, John (1709), Thomas (1711), Jane (1712), Ann (1714) and Mary (1717), were all baptised by the Rev. John Olive, successor to Thomas Barnard at the Westgate Meeting House with which the family was to be closely associated until the middle of the 19th century.

In 1719 the Westgate Dissenters bought the property in which they held their meetings and among the trustees named in the deed is Richard Ridge of Stoneham, yeoman. The chapel is of interest as it still retains some of the architectural features of the original 16th-century building which was the town house of Sir Henry Goring. Adjoining it is a small house in Bull Lane where Tom Paine resided when he was writing *The Age of Reason*. In 1735 John, the second son of Richard, was married and in order that the newly married couple should have the use of Upper Stoneham Farm, Richard and his wife together with his unmarried children, William, Thomas, Jane, Anne and Mary, moved to a house he had just built in the parish of Hamsey. William duly recorded in his Book of Memorandoms: 'And in the year 1735 was the House Called new Tullys well Built it was reared Agust 1. The Healing of it was Finish. September ye 20; 1735 we Removed from Stoneham into it December ye 2: 1735'.

The following year Stephen Ridge of Chailey died and having carried out the provisions of his father's will in respect of his niece, Sarah, Richard of Stoneham became the freeholder of Woodbrookes Farm, Chailey. The Deed Poll of Release[43] shows that he left his brother's widow in possession of the farm presumably for the duration of her natural life.

In the same year, 1736, his youngest son, Thomas, died at the age of 25. An account of the funeral was carefully recorded by William as follows: 'SOMETHING OF THE MANNER AND CHARGE OF THE BURYAL OF MY BROTHER THOMAS who dyed ye 9th February 1735/6 and buryed ye 13 being Fryday. Viz: gave Gloves & favours to 6 young men that caryed him from the hearse to the ground Viz: William Crawley: William Boys: William Packham:

The first gentleman

Joseph Attersoll: Richard Read: Cruttenden Weller. [All six bearers were relatives by marriage.] his Father and Mother Brothers and Sisters had Cloaths and Gloves & hatbands. None of his Aunts were here his Unkels that were here had Gloves and hatbands & Servants and workmen had Gloves bought one Gallon of Red wine at $6^s 6^d p^r$. gallon & a galon and a half of White at 5^s 6^d gallon and that was about half drank: The Coffin lined within and without but no plate cost 30^s. The hearse Cost one Guinea had him of Thomas Frind. Sergeant Hamans horses John Read Searve the Funeral.'

It would appear from this extract that arrangements for the funeral were in the hands of William and the care with which he records details, particularly of money matters, characterised him throughout his long life. At this time, his father, although not yet 60 years old, recognised William's ability and retired from active farming to become a 'gentleman', This is indicated by a letter of Attorney[44] dated 16 May 1738, referring to some copyhold lands 'occupied by Richard Ridge, gent.'. He probably divided his time between Tully Wells and Lewes since a further trust deed of Westgate Meeting House made in 1751 cites him as 'of Hamsey', whilst a list of pew-holders[45] in St. Michael's Church, Lewes, gives his address as 89 High Street.

In 1742 a young Scottish Minister, the Rev. Ebenezer Johnston succeeded to the pastorship of Westgate Meeting House. William's account of his ordination, written with his usual attention to detail, throws some light on the conduct of the chapel services and on the members of the congregation.

'Something of the way and maner that Mr. Ebenezer Johnston was Ordained at Lewes ye 21: July 1742 Viz Mr. Mason of Darking began with a Short prayer and read the 34th of Ezekiel the 10 first Vearses of the third Chap of ye first of Timothy and 2th of Titus and then Said Something in A way of Preface then read the Churches invitation which was signed by Richard Ridge, Tho Barret, William Attersol, Tho Davy, Cruttenden Weller and I believe William English and after reading he Asked them for they with Some others of the Church sat together wether they did not allow of the Invitation if thay did they should make Some sighn as by holding up their hands which they did and then he asked

Mr. Johnston wether he excepted of the invitation the wich he Declared he did then we sung the 10th hymn of ye 1th Book then Mr. Johnston of Wisbich Brother to the ordained went in the pulpit and prayed and then Mr Jinnings of London Preached A Sermon on the 2 Corinthians 4:5 and then Mr Sammuel Snashal of Newington went into the pulpit and asked Mr Johnston to read his beleif the which also Mr Johnston Read and then Mr Snashal came down to the Seat where the following Ministers were to wit Mr Jinnings, Docter Dodridge, Mr Johnston of Wisbich, Mr Dear of Burwash, Mr Duke of Brightelmstone, Mr Whatkins of Lewis, Mr Mason of Darking, Mr Whittle of Battle, Mr Chantler of Turners Hill and there Mr Snashal with most of the Rest Layed there hands on the head of Mr. Johnston as he Kneeled and Mr Snashal prayed over him And then Docter Dodridge of Northampton [A great Nonconformist Divine, Principal of the Northampton Academy where Ebenezer Johnston had studied.] went into the pulpit and gave the charge and then Sung the 1st and two Last Verses of the 128 hymn of ye 1st Book and then Mr. Dear went in pulpit and concluded with A prayer. Whole service was about four hours and A half began about A Qurter befor Eeleven and ended about A Qurter after three. The Aforewriting is as near as I could call to mind after I came home the Same day at Night. William Ridge.

After the Ordination there was a Dinner provided for the Ministers at Cruttenden Wellers by the Joynt Charge of Several and Dyned the 11 Ministers before mentioned and Mr Butten of Rye, Mr Beach of Lewes, Mr Marshall who came with Dr Dodridge and Docter Avery and Thomas Davy Apothecary.'

William Attersoll, Cruttenden Weller and Samuel Snashal were all related to the Ridges by marriage and in the following year the Rev. Ebenezer Johnston himself joined the family when he married Mary, the youngest daughter of Richard Ridge.

Richard, the first gentleman in the family, died at Lewes in November, 1755 and was interred in the new family vault in the churchyard of St. Michael's, Lewes. In his will he left all his household goods and an annuity of £24 to his wife

Ann, an annuity of £6 to his sister Sarah Pope and legacies of £100 each to his two grandchildren Elizabeth Ridge and Stephen Weller. His executor and residual legatee was, as might be expected, his eldest son William whilst his youngest son, John, at Upper Stoneham received some 24 acres of copyhold land in the manor of Framfield, his mother's birthplace.

JOHN RIDGE OF STONEHAM
Gentleman. 1710-1778

THE YOUNGEST SON of Richard Ridge appears to have been an extrovert with a flair for enjoying life. He was a good farmer because there is no evidence to the contrary in his elder brother's 'Memorandom Book' and there is little doubt that any serious departure from the family way of life would have been faithfully recorded in great detail. John married Elizabeth Cockle in London on 29 October 1735. A son John was born in 1736 (he died of smallpox in 1752 at the age of 16) and a daughter Elizabeth in 1737. Less than two years later, Elizabeth Cockle died in childbirth. John remained a widower until about 1754 when he married Ann Chairman. There were no children of this marriage and the only information about her is from an entry in the 'Memorandom Book': 'December 26: 1773. Sister Ridge (she was married July 21: 17----?) of Kingston dyed Jany 3 put in the Vault in St. Michaels aged 54'.

There seems to have been little in common between John and his brother William who only mentions him twice; once in connection with the great drought of 1743-4, 'Brother Ridge at Stoneham forced to drive his Oxen down to Lower Stoneham Spring dick' and finally a brief but detailed note of his death: 'November 29: 1778 John Ridge son of Richard Ridge dyed at Greenwich and put in the Vault at St. Michaels Decm: 8 1778. Aged 68 years 8 months 28 days. Born February 18th 1709/10'. On the other hand John appears to have found

Fig. 3   Journey into Kent, 1744

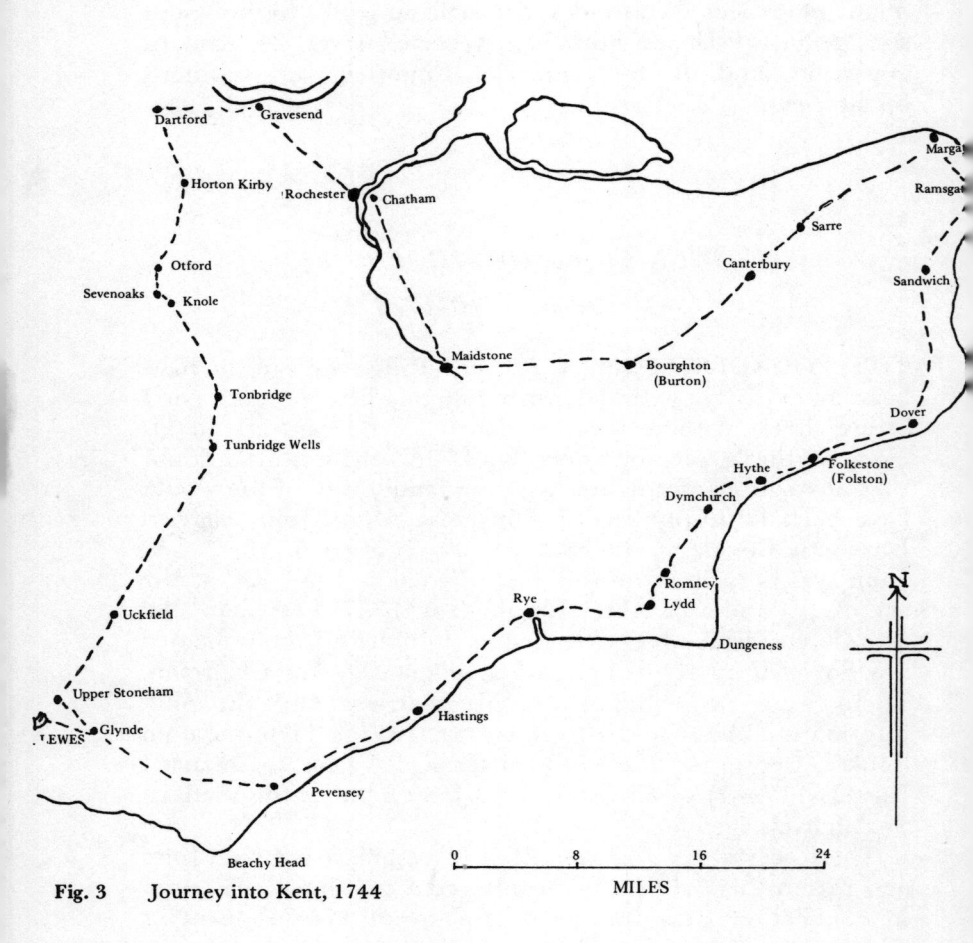

The first gentleman

a good companion in his brother-in-law, Ebenezer Johnston and in 1744 the two of them together with a Mr. Palmer of Ranscombe left Stoneham to make a journey into the neighbouring county of Kent. The journal[46] kept in great detail by Ebenezer Johnston gives some insight into the character of John Ridge and shows that the writer was no stern Puritan divine but was blessed with the Scot's pawky sense of humour.

July 23. Mounted our horses five minutes after six in ye morning, called at ye Maiden Head in Uckfield where we drank a glass of wine. Reached Tunbridge Wells about eleven where we dined & fed our horses at ye Angel. Came on to Tunbridge Town. Made a short stay there, put up at ye Rose and Crown. Went to see ye old Castle & Mr. Hocker's Vineyard, where we had an agreable Prospect. Went from thence towards Knowle, entered ye Duke of Dorset's Park at ye White Hart on Sevenoke Common. Surprised at our first entrance with a most beautiful and pleasing prospect. Saw several Deers, & a Squirrel with a White Tail which mightily took with us & occasioned some mirth. Lost our way in ye Park but ye riding so pleasant that our wandering was sufficiently made up thereby. At last we came to the Duke's house, a noble and ancient Building in which its said yr are upward of Seven Hundred Rooms. Then we came to Sevenoke, lodged at ye Crown Inn. The Town is but indifferent ill accommodated for Water. This evening Mr. Palmer Bought a Pair of Steel Spurrs & I had a lash put on my Whip.

July 24. Rose in ye morning between five and six o'clock took a walk before Breakfast to Mr. Delamare's Silk-Mill and was pleasantly entertained with ye curious & ingenious Works but were not admitted to see ye Chief Engine or Wheel by which all ye rest are turned. Proceeded on our journey and got a Mug of Beer at Aynesford. At a Mile before Ottford to Houghton-Kirby ye Road was exceeding stony. We got to Dartford about Eleven, drank a Pint of Wine at ye Cock. There we saw two Ostriches, a Male & Female and two Ostrich Eggs etc. At Gravesend dined at Mr. Rays. After dinner Mr. Palmer and Mr. Ridge went over to Tilbury Fort but tho't it a mean Fortification. We drank tea at Mr. Rays. Afterwards Mr. Boorman, Mr. Ridge and Miss Cook of Wisbeach walked up to Windmill-Hill together, took a Prospect of ye Country round about. But Mr. Ridge seemed much better pleased with ye company of ye Lady he was with. He seemed under some concern at Mr. Boorman's presence. Whether Him and ye Lady had any private discourse together is uncertain, but perhaps we may judge something of it by yr winding up of her Gold Watch, perhaps at ye other side of ye Mill to where Mr. Boorman was. This part of our Journal we must acknowledge to be somewhat obscure, but its no wonder, since affairs of this Nature are generally unknown to others at ye Beginning of them at least. Mr. Ridge himself is ye best expositor upon it. On towards Rochester, drank a pot of Beer at ye Sign of K. Henry on Gad's Hill. Ye Cathedral is not so mean as was represented to us, newly repaired & beautified in ye inside. The Bishop's Palace a most despicable Place, more like a Jail yn a Prelates Palace.

July 25. Rose about Six, had but an indifferent night's rest. This morning were shaved. Breakfasted on Cold Mutton. Made Chatham Dock on our way to Maidstone. Our Horses were taken care of at ye Gate. We were had before Commodore Brown (whom we were glad to see). He enquired of us whence we were, & having inform'd him, He told us we were extremely Wellcome. We went on Board ye *Royal George,* a First Rate from whence we saw Cheerness, afterwards went to ye Gunn Yard where we saw ye Brass Gunns belonging to ye *Royal George.* For Maidstone between ten & eleven, drank a mug of beer ye Blue Bell in ye way. Dined at ye Bull in Maidstone. Between two & three proceeded on our way to Canterbury. Drank half a Pint of Wine at ye Cock in Burton. At ye end of this street met with a Prating Fellow who accompanied us most of the way to Canterbury.

July 26. Went to see ye Cathedral. Many curious things in it, & remains of Antiquity. Ridge and I went up ye Steeple and we drank a glass of Wine at Saar and reached Margate at twelve, & then Ramsgate, at which last mentioned Place we were told yr was upwards of 300 Masters of Ships that lived in ye town. A new Meeting House built in it, Mr. Spence from ye Orkneys Minister of it. About 3 or 4 miles from Canterbury

Plate 1: *Common fields at Firle*

Plate 2: *Burnt House Farm, Fletching*

Plate 3: *Ovingdean Church*

Plate 4: *Iford Church*

Plate 5: *Tudor Farmhouse, Iford*

Plate 6: *Woodbrookes Farm, Chailey*

Plate 7: *Upper Stoneham, South Malling*

Plate 8: *Tully Wells, Hamsey*

Plate 9: *Alciston Place*

Plate 10: *Alciston Place, Tithe Barn*

Plate 11: *St. Michael's Churchyard, Lewes; Ridge and Johnston vaults*

Plate 12: *St. Anne's House, 143 High Street, Lewes (now demolished)*

At the Law Day holden for the Town and Borough of Lewes this Tenth day of October in the Thirteenth Year of the Reign of our Sovereign Lord George the Third by the Grace of God of Great Britain France and Ireland King Defender of the Faith and so forth, And in the Year of our Lord 1772 By ~~Thos Lully~~ Esquires Steward there were Chosen for Constables and Headboroughs as follows Viz.

Stephen Heaver } Constables
William Ridge

John Hide } Headboroughs
George Edmunds

The Accounts of Stephen Heaver and William Ridge the aforesaid Constables made and given in to ———— Richard Read and John Hibb new Constables and to the Jury the twenty fifth day of October is ~~at~~ One Thousand seven hundred and Seventy three. Viz.

The Charge.

The said Stephen Heaver and William Ridge do Charge themselves with several Sums of Money received by them and which are particularly mentioned and entered in the other Book of Accounts Amounting in the whole to the Sum of ....

£ 24 – 13 – 0

The Discharge.

The said Stephen Heaver and William Ridge do Discharge themselves by several Payments and Disbursements particularly mentioned in the other Book of Accounts Amounting in the whole to the Sum of ......

19 – 10 – 7

Ballance in hand to be paid to the next Constable   5 – 2 – 5

24 – 13 – 0

And likewise the said Stephen Heaver and William Ridge have delivered into the hands of the said New Constables in the presence of the Jury the several Deeds, Bonds Surrenders, Writings and Evidences Together with the several Books, Utensils and other things hereinafter mentioned belonging to the said Borough. (That is to say)

1) Some Writings in the Old Box thought proper to be preserved —
2) Also Henry White and his wife and Thomas Brett and his Wife their Mortgage of Land called Godleys to Mr. Richard Bernard for one Hundred Pounds Dated 26. December 1701. with Bond and Indentures of ~~fine~~
3) Also Mr. Bernards Assignment of the same to the Lewes Constables Dated 4th February 1703.
4) Also an Appointment of New Trustees for the same Dated 2d January 1729.
5) Also Henry Whites Sale of the same to the Constables of Lewes Dated 4th February 1703.
6) Also Mr. Michells and others Conveyance by Lease and Release of the same Dated 27 & 28 July 1771.
7) Also one Deed of Feoffment for the Alms houses in the Parish of All Saints — (missing)
8) Also four Parchment Deeds concerning Blunts Houses in Saint Michaels, and how the Rents are disposed of —
9) Also Mr. Court and Doctor Tabors Bond for £50. Dated 16. October 1707 —
10) Also Six Parchment Deeds concerning the Clock house —
11) Also One Deed concerning Lewes Bridge —
12) Also One writing concerning the Quart and Pint Measures.

Also the Town Bell now in the Custody of Saml. Durrant Esqr.

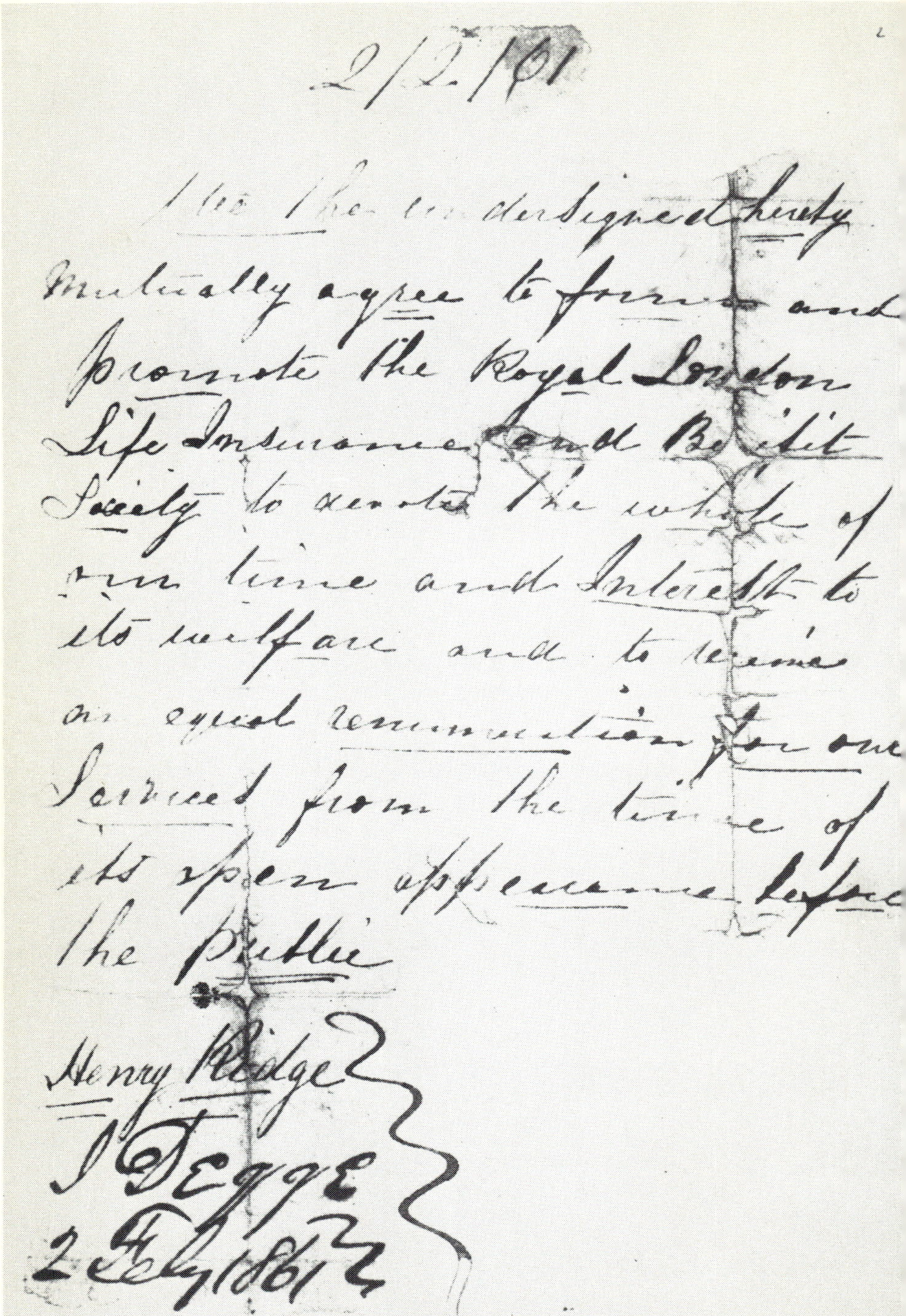

2/2/101

We the undersigned hereby mutually agree to form and promote the Royal London Life Insurance and Benefit Society to devote the whole of our time and Interest to its welfare and to receive an equal remuneration for our Services from the time of its open appearance before the Public

Henry Ridge
J Degge
2 Feby 1861

Plate 14: 'We the undersigned...'

The first gentleman

towards Margate we saw Canary Seed which we had never seen before, & afterwards we saw more of it The people seem to be more respectful to travellers, even Children seem to be taught to bow to Persons. Drank a Pot of Beer at Story, came to Sandwich, went on to Deal. Made a stop for about an Hour. This Day in ye morning Commodore Byng* Hoisted his Flag on Board ye *Winchester* a 50 Gunn Shippe, there was also in ye Downs a 60 Gunn Shipp, as also another of forty. At Dover we saw a French Privateer brought into ye Harbour by ye Dover Privateer. Ye Lieutenant of Franch Man is an Irishman, and, they said, put in irons. Ye Captain of Her was shot thro' ye Jaws. She carried sixty men. One boat full of Prisoners we saw. Tho' this was but a small Privateer yet she had done Merchant's shipps considerable damage, & had taken five or six of ym it was reported a little before she was taken herself.

July 27. We saw several French Prizes in ye Harbour. & many French Prisoners in ye Town. We met with but indifferent treatment at ye Ship where we lodged here. Mr. Ridge much disturbed with ye Rats & Mice inasmuch that he was obliged to leave his Bed. This morning Breakfasted on Neats-Tongue, afterwards took horses. On our journey we passed through Folston, came to Hith, drank at ye Pelican, had a pleasant ride along ye shore thro' Dim-Church reached Romney about eleven o'clock, baited near half an hour at ye Rose & Crown yr. & were civilly entertained for our Money. Came to Lid before one. Saw several Shipps as we rode along ye Shore, & one large Fleet at a distance which we took for Men of War. Dined at ye George at Lid, a great company of Smugglers there, known in ye house & in ye town to be such, and were as impudent and bold as tho' yr were no Laws in being agst them. Proceeded on our Journey, ye road to Rye not so difficult as we apprehended, got to Rye over ye Ferry, about five of ye evening, baited at ye George where we found ye Gentlemen of the town met together to consult about fitting out a Privateer from thence to cruise on ye Coasts of Spain. A little after six went on our way to

---

* Afterwards Admiral Byng who was court-martialled and shot on board the *Monarch* in 1757 as a scapegoat for the Administration.

Hastings. Met Mr. Burton* about five miles from ye Town. Drank with him. He had lost one of his Silver Spurrs. A most difficult and intricate Road from Rye. At Hastings, lodged at ye Swan. A Prating Maid in ye House. A great Noise in it occasioned by a Scotchman's imprudent zeal for his Country and an English Man's foolish contempt for it. Went to bed about Eleven, slept well & rose a little after four, which brings us to 28 July and last day of our journey. Bought some shrimps on ye Sea Shore, had ym dressed and boiled at ye Shipp & breakfasted on ym again. Passed thro' Pevensey on our way to Lewes, drank at a House on ye top of a Hil. Then Glin where Mr. Ridge left us. Mr. Palmer & I went on to Ranscombe. I drank a Glass of Beer there and ate a piece of Biscuit. Here I left Mr. Palmer. I went on to Lewes which I reached a little before two in good health.

Ebenezer Johnston remained at Westgate Meeting House until 1782 when he retired to Brighton. He died in 1791 at the age of 71 and lies buried in St. Michael's Churchyard next to the family vault of the Ridges.

It is interesting to note that of his eight children the eldest, William, was minister at Westgate from 1811-1817[47] and his second son, Ebenezer[48] lived at Barbican House (since 1908 the Headquarters of the Sussex Archaeological Society) until his death in 1826.

John Ridge was still farming at Upper Stoneham in 1755 but in a Chapel trust deed of 1757 he is described as 'of Kingston near Lewes, gentleman'. It gives rise to some speculation as to how he was able to retire at the early age of 48 because on the death of his grandfather in 1755 the lease of Upper Stoneham became vested in his brother William. Round about this time his daughter Elizabeth married Robert Maitland, a West India Merchant of Greenwich whose father, Robert Maitland the elder, had recently purchased the Manor of Kingston[49] and it is highly probable that John Ridge managed the estates until his death in 1778. The fact that the first recorded Court held by Robert and Elizabeth Maitland

---

* Mr. *Butten* mentioned in William Ridge's account of the Ordination of Ebenezer Johnston (p.32).

The first gentleman

was in 1779 has given rise to the suggestion that John Ridge was Lord of the Manor of Kingston and that on his death it passed to Elizabeth Maitland, his sole heiress. There is, however, no documentary evidence to support this claim and it is more likely that Robert Maitland the elder died at about the same time as John Ridge, the Manorial Rights passing to Elizabeth's husband, his eldest son and heir.

CHAPTER VII

THE MAN OF PURPOSE

WILLIAM RIDGE OF LEWES
Gentleman. 1709-1802

WILLIAM RIDGE was only 14 months older than his brother John, but no two men could have differed so much both in temperament and conduct. At the age of 29 John was a widower whilst William did not marry until he was 49, the year in which his brother left Upper Stoneham and settled at Kingston near Lewes in semi-retirement. Ebenezer Johnston's journal shows that John was a sociable person not unresponsive to feminine company and he probably had friends among the congregation of the Westgate Meeting House of which he was a trustee. William, although attending the chapel and recording some of the meetings in his 'Memorandom Book', was never a trustee. His association with the Meeting House was probably inspired more by filial duty than by religious conviction for after the death of his father in 1755 it was never mentioned again. There is no evidence that he made any purely social contacts and although in his will he refers to 'friends Saml. Snashall of Lewes and Joseph Ridge of Iford', the former was the husband of his wife's niece and the latter his wife's nephew, both selected to act as trustees.

All the ambitions of his forebears to further the prosperity of the family were crystallised in this one man. Anything which had no bearing on his sole aim in life was trivial and unworthy of consideration. Important things were those which had a purpose and if they could be expressed in figures, so much the better. His 'Memorandom Book' was for his personal

The man of purpose

use only and therefore he disregarded such trivialities as spelling, the rules of grammar and punctuation but was meticulous about facts as the following extracts show:

'May 20 : 1732 I Bought a Watch of Mr. Thomas Barrett that cost me five pound. of Mr. James Chaters make Number 897 the name and number as tis Set Down.
Within Side Counterfeited as Near as I could Jannuary ye 2nd 1740/1 as follows: Jam^S Chater^V 897. LONDON.
Observe the Crotchet between Chater and 897 is caused by fyling of Something.' Some four years later he wrote:
'Counterfeited again August ye 22: 1745 Jam^S Chater^V 897 London.' Followed by: 'Within Side of Iner Case wrote with A fork Hamsey April ye 23: 1748, W. Ridge.'

Another entry reads: 'Observe always before December ye 25: 1763 I Signed My Name thus *William Ridge* ever Since thus *Wm. Ridge.*'

In his later years he was still preoccupied with detail as shown by his concern for his money-bags.

'August 27: 1782 I had 4 Yellow Mony Bags Made Marked thus Wm Ridge Marked Within Side All one Size Observe the
      82
W began at the Seam and the 8 right under the g the 82 for the Date'.

'Some White Bags before marked Wm Ridge Observe the 1
      1776
Just under Last tip of W and top of 6 Just under last stroke of R'.

'December ye 8: 1785 I had 6 Mony Bags 3 White and 3 Yellow all Marked within Side thus Wm Ridge 1 under first
      1785
tip of W, 7 under last and 5 under first tip of R'.

Even when walking back to Lewes after a visit to Upper Stoneham he had to satisfy himself about the most economical route!

'A MEMORANDUM. May 3: 1753 I paced and timed from were the ways part to go to Dr. Russels Bridge And the Clift A top of Malling Hill to Lewes Market House

    By Doctors Bridge   26 minutes
                                       2240 paces

By the Clift   21 minutes
                                1840 paces
The Difference is about 5.5 to 4.5'

As the decimal system was still some 50 years ahead, the last figures probably represent minutes and seconds! It is quite in keeping with his character that the 'Memorandom Book' has an account of the Land Tax per pound from 1743 to 1785. It varied between 3d. and 4d. with three low years (1753, 54, 55) at 2d.!

Events outside his immediate locality were of no interest and although during his long life there were wars with Spain and France, the Jacobite Risings, the French Revolution and the loss of the American Colonies, they are not mentioned in his notes except for one entry which begins:

'January ye 9: 1739/40 A Fast kept on Account of war with Spain' [The War of Jenkin's Ear] 'kept in Lewis in the uper Meeting house . . .'. On the other hand material catastrophes which affected the people of Lewes and its immediate surroundings are recorded in great detail. A vivid description of the great frost which lasted from December 1739 until May 1740 contains a passing reference to places further afield when he writes:

'Some places expecially in Kent a Snow knee deep the Frost was very bad at London the Thames was freest up So that people and horses went acrost.'

Much more important was the effect of the severe winter on the local economy. Some notes added at a later date refer to the price of wheat following the great frost. Before the harvest of 1740 it rose to £15 or £16 per load and 'Almost as Much ever Since to this time January ye 2: 1741/2 but a little before Harvest it fell to Near five pound the Load and it as Continued to be very Low ever since. It tis but four pound ten the Load January ye 1: 1743/4.'

Excessive rainfall in the Ouse catchment area can cause serious flooding in the low lying land around Lewes and was, before the era of the Ouse River Authority, of grave concern to farmers.

'The year 1768 was very wet later part of Harvest So wet as to Spoil the Corn the most as I ever new and on September the 21 there was a large Flood as flowed up to the Corner of

Bridge Coffe Coach House and So Continued large Floods till the 3^d December when there was a Flood that flowed in every lower room of the Bear and about half way up the Iron Ring that hangs on the warehouse on the North east Corner of the Bridge Suppose to be almost as high as at any time.'

'Novem^{br} 12: 1773 A Flood flowed over Ring & Staple of North East Corner of Clift Bridge and up to 10th Brick below Copping Brick of Corner of Bear House the Bear being new Built and Raised Since 1768.'

'December 4th 1779 Flood Flowed up half way up 15th Brick as above.'

There is no doubt that William Ridge had an enquiring turn of mind and was a great reader (his library is mentioned in his will, appendix p.70) but it is safe to conjecture that his books would be of an instructive or informative nature and that novels would be excluded as 'purposeless'.

His observations on comets show that he was not unacquainted with the heavenly bodies and he probably possessed some of the descriptive books on Astronomy which were gaining popularity towards the end of the 18th century.

'September ye 2: 1769 I See a Comet about 3 o Clock in the Morning about ½ as far South of Bulls Eye as Bulls Eye is from the Pleides . . . Tail about as long as tis between Pleides and Bulls Eye.

September 4 Saw him again and then he was much more East than before being as far and half as far from Bulls Eye as Bulls Eye is from the Pleides . . .'.

Again, in another account of 'A Blazing Star', he says: 'February the 9 being a Clear Night I see the Star again and he was Vastly increased in Bigness appearing to be as big as Jupiter but red like Mars . . . He had gained of the fixed Stars [the Pleiades] about an hour and Seemed a Little bearing to the South of them and his tail seemed to bear round to the North Star More.'

Included in his 'Memorandom Book' are 'A true pitch for Rafters of an house', the results of the Lewes and Sussex Elections in 1774, a note on the date of the invention of guns and of printing and a number of Puzzling Questions' of which the following is an example.

'A Butcher went to wey A pound of Meat and he had Lost

all his weights except a Stone which weyed just 40 pound he had a fansy wether he could not break off Just a pound off from him and in doing of it he broke it in 4 pieces but So Nisely that with them he could wey any number of pounds from 1^{lb} to 40^{lb} I Desire to know what weights them 4 pieces must be.
Answer 1^{lb} 2^{lb} 9^{lb} and 27^{lb}.'

There can be little doubt that during the lifetime of his father William devoted himself whole-heartedly to the management of the large estate which he eventually inherited in 1755 (Will of Richard Ridge, 1755, appendix, p.69). There would have been no change in his methods which were both efficient and profitable, but he was now faced with the problem of succession. Should he die unmarried the property would pass to his brother John who had no male heir, his only son having died of small-pox in 1752. On the death of John the Ridge estates, so carefully nurtured and now at the peak of prosperity, would go to John's daughter, Elizabeth, and out of the family on her marriage. At all costs the family must retain the property and the only solution was for William himself to marry and ensure that he had male heirs. No doubt this proposition was given the same careful consideration that would be given to buying or selling land. His wife must be young and healthy, capable of bearing sufficient children to ensure at least one boy. She should be of a wealthy family so that her dowry would add to the family property and if possible she should have a sense of purpose in maintaining the priority of the family.

With his curious singleness of purpose William weighed the pros and cons of all the eligible ladies and finally, two years after the death of his father, made his selection. Sarah Ridge was 26, the daughter of Benjamin Ridge of Iford, gentleman, and above all she was of the same stock.

The marriage took place at Iford on 6 December 1757 and in November of the following year their first child was born. It was no doubt somewhat of a disappointment to William that it was a girl, although he makes no complaint in his 'Memorandum Book':

'Novem 19: 1758 A Daughter born to William Ridge and Sarah his wife December ye 11: Baptiz^d by Mr. Johnston and named Sarah.' Fortunately for his peace of mind the next four children were sons and although two died in infancy, Richard (1762) and Benjamin (1764) grew to manhood.

William's mother died in 1764 and her death is recorded accurately but without emotion.

'April ye 21: 1764 Ann Wife of Richard Ridge dyed Aged 82 years 5 months 27 days dyed about 7 in even And Buryed ye 26 in the Vault in St. Michaels'.

Round about the time of his marriage William established himself in Lewes and began to interest himself in town affairs. Lewes, unlike the majority of the old towns in England, was not incorporated as a borough by Royal Charter. In the early days this was understandable as it was the headquarters of the Barony of Lewes and administration would have been from the Castle. This medieval system persisted long after the power of the baron had dwindled to that of a superior landlord. John Rowe writing in 1662 says:

'Within the Borough of Lewes, time beyond all memory, the Law Day or View of Frankpledge is kept but once a year viz:- the first Monday after Michaelmas at which Court are chosen those Officers following:- Two Constables, two Headboroughs, one Scavenger, one Pound Keeper, one Searcher of Leather, one Clerk of the Wheat Market, one Clerk of the Butchery, one Clerk of Spars and Withs and Ale Houses.' Election of the Constables was by 'The Twelve', 'A Society of the wealthier and discreeter sort of the Townsfolk.' All subordinate appointments were made by the Constables. It was not until 1881 that Lewes became a Municipal Borough and the Senior High Constable was elected as the first Mayor.

William Ridge was not the first member of the family to be elected to 'The Twelve'. In 1727 Thomas Ridge was one of the Headboroughs and active in town affairs until 1732. The name of John Ridge of Southover, tanner, appears in the Town Books in 1735, in 1739 as Headborough (with Cruttenden Weller) and in 1741 as one of the Constables. With his fellow Constable, Richard Turner, he raised by public subscription the sum of £421 9s. 1d. for the erection of a Pest House. Both John and Thomas were members of a cadet branch of the family, descended from Thomas Ridge of the Cliffe (see p.26).

The first mention of William Ridge in the Town Books is in 1762 when he was a Headborough and signed as one of the Twelve.

The following extract from the Town Books for 1765 shows that people in the 18th century were just as concerned about the rising costs of local government as they are today:

'8th November Law Day by adjournment at ye Town Hall . . . and Publick Notice having been given by Henry Verrall and James Weston the Constables . . . by their Town Cryer . . . that the usual Town Tax would be taken into consideration at this Time and Place and whereas it hath been represented that divers persons within the said Borough have given out that they will not contribute or pay their assessments towards the Town Charges and other Duties. We the said Constables and other Inhabitants [i.e. the Twelve] of the said Borough do with unanimous and joint consent that if any Suits at Law arise . . . we will contribute and bear our parts of all such Charges . . . in Maintenance of the Rights, Immunities and Customs of the said Borough. In Witness . . .'.

Here follow a number of signatures, presumably of the Twelve, including Wm Ridge and Joseph Ridge. Joseph Ridge, surgeon, lived at 80 High Street, Lewes (now the showrooms of the South Eastern Electrictiy Board.) He was married to Elizabeth Snashall and was brother-in-law to William Ridge whom he outlived by 14 years.

Six years later the Constables and the Twelve found it necessary to emphasise once again their right to levy town taxes and the entry in the Town Books reads:

'4th Day of March 1771. Resolved Constables and Jury at the Court Leet of Law Day chosen shall and do continue to have power to make and collect a Tax for defraying the necessary Expences of the Borough aforesaid.'

In the following year Stephen Hewer, barber, and William Ridge, gentleman, were elected Constables and it is noticeable that the signature of the latter shows signs of infirmity. This is more pronounced three years later when, as one of the Twelve, he signed the following minute:

'Meeting of the Inhabitants of the Borough 10th November 1775. 3/- per week to Richard Stacey for looking after and keeping well air'd the Pest House . . . when their are no patients therein.'

The man of purpose

This is the last time that William's name appears in the Town Books and although he was only 67 he appears to have dropped out of public life. He may have suffered from arthritis which would make writing more difficult as time went on and this supposition has some support from the gradual deterioration of his handwriting in the 'Memorandom Book' which he kept going for another 10 years. In 1798 he conveyed Woodbrookes Farm to his son Benjamin and as the deed is attested by his seal and mark he was by that time incapable of writing. Whatever physical disability it was that afflicted him, his mental powers remained unimpaired and he was able to add a very clear codicil to his will on the day that he died (Appendix p.73).

In 1784 William's daughter Sarah was married. She was 26 years of age and the choice of a husband must have presented her father with the same problem that beset him with the female succession of his brother John. He solved it in the same way that he had arranged his own marriage — within the family. His choice was William Ridge of Alciston, nephew of his wife. It is rather confusing to be confronted with two William Ridges married to two Sarah Ridges and William of Alciston was faced with the alternatives of addressing William of Lewes either as 'uncle' or 'father'! Taking into account the disparity in their ages and the austerity of his father-in-law, he probably settled for 'sir'!

Court Farm, Alciston, is a fine example of a hall house and originally belonged to Battle Abbey. At the Dissolution of the Monasteries it passed to the Gage family of Firle, in whose hands it still remains. The property, sometimes called the Manor House or Alciston Place, was leased to William Ridge. Writing in 1827 Horsfield says:

'The Manor House or Alciston Place was occupied by an ancestor [Sir John Gage, 1585] of the present Lord Gage . . . it was afterwards tenanted by Mr. William Ridge who, together with his own extensive property in the neighbourhood used for many years the Manor Farm. During his occupation Alciston Place was considerably improved and modernised.'

Of the two sons of William Ridge of Lewes, Benjamin, the younger, was a facsimile of his father. A good business man, imbued with the sense of family priority and taking readily to his father's way of life, he was a Benjamin indeed. The elder boy, Richard, took after his uncle John of Stoneham. He liked company, made friends (many of them unsuitable by his father's standards) and did not regard as his primary aim in life the advancement of the family. This would be an unforgivable sin in the eyes of William and in 1786 he wrote a letter to Richard (then aged 24) urging him to mend his ways under threat of disinheritance. Whether their differences were due to a clash of temperaments or whether Richard was in fact sowing his wild oats is not known. At any rate, the letter seems to have had no effect and five years later, when Richard married Ann Turner, a tanner's daughter of Fletching, all contact with the family seems to have ceased.

In 1795 Benjamin married Sarah Palmer of Lewes, a match of which his father thoroughly approved and two years later William made a will in which Benjamin was named as his heir and sole executor.

William Ridge died on 11 April 1802, a very rich man. His personal estate was sworn to be not in excess of £5,000, a very large sum by modern standards. To his wife he left his house (St. Anne's House, 143 High Street; formerly occupied by John Rowe), all his household effects including plate, linen, china and library of books, £1,200 and an annuity of £50. To his daughter Sarah, wife of William Ridge of Alciston a legacy of £700. His philosophy of family priority remained with him to the end, for although he had disinherited Richard he appointed his son-in-law William, Samuel Snashall of Lewes and Joseph Ridge of Iford as trustees to manage certain of his estates in Ringmer and to pay the rents and profits therefrom to Richard and Ann his wife. After their demise the money was to be applied to the benefit of their children until the youngest attained the age of 21. Then if both parents were dead, the estates were to be sold to the best purchaser and the proceeds of the sale divided between Richard's children. A proviso makes it clear that should Richard attempt to raise money by selling or assigning his rights under his father's will, then the trustees were to treat him as dead and apply all the monies to his wife and children. The residue of the estate, both real and personal, was left to Benjamin. This will (Will of William Ridge, 1802,

The man of purpose

appendix p.70) epitomises William's way of life and is a fitting, if lengthy, epitaph.

Benjamin made the final entry in the 'Memorandom Book':
'He died 11th Apl. 1802 Aged 93. Buried St. Michaels 16 Apl. 1802.'

CHAPTER VIII

'THE OLD ORDER CHANGETH...'

BENJAMIN RIDGE OF CHAILEY
Gentleman. 1764-1849

WHEN WILLIAM RIDGE finally established himself at St. Anne's House in Lewes, he presumably disposed of Tully Wells as the Land Tax Record for 1780 shows that property 'late Ridges' in the parish of Hamsey was occupied by James Ellis and owned by Thomas W. Partington Esq.* On reaching his majority the younger son, Benjamin, was installed by his father at Woodbrookes Farm for in a Westgate Chapel trust deed of 1785 he is described as 'of Chailey, gentleman', It is quite likely that he had sufficient property to manage without having to work himself.

There is no doubt that the younger son carried out his duties with success and after his marriage to Sarah Palmer in 1795 he was regarded as the inevitable successor to William. Benjamin and Sarah had only two children, Mary, born about 1797 and Sarah, a year or two later.

About this time William conveyed the lease of Woodbrookes[50] and some other lands to Benjamin for the term of 21 years at an annual rental of £90, a clear indication that the old gentleman although just over 90 was still quite capable of tying up the loose ends of a business deal. In his will of 1797, he had left the freeholds of these particular lands to his wife for life and Benjamin as the occupier was to pay his mother an annuity of £50 out of the estates. He safeguarded his son's interests by the 21-year lease as a reason-

* Thomas Walter Partington was Steward (ie. Town Clerk) to the Twelve when William Ridge was chosen as Constable in 1772.

able estimate of his wife's expectancy of life, (actually it proved to be 14 years) and on the other hand, if the annuity or rent charges were not paid within 21 days of the due date, his widow could enter and distrain!

Meanwhile Benjamin was dealing in property on his own account. On 1 December 1798[51] he bought from Robert Chester Cooper, a brewer of Lewes, the lease of the *Swan Inn* and lands at Falmer and in the following March[52] he disposed of the property (no doubt at a profit) to Thomas Pelham of Stanmer. The Land Tax Returns for Fletching in 1799 show that he was the owner of some 28 acres in that Parish, in particular Burnt House Farm.

In 1802 on presentment of the death of his father to the Court of the Manor of Allington,[53] Benjamin was admitted to the copyhold lands of Lower Barn and of Wickham and Rowley in the Parish of St. John sub Castro and the whole of the family estates came under his control on the death of his mother in 1811. Most of her household effects, jewellery and books were left to her daughter Sarah whilst ready money, securities and the remainder of her personal estate were divided equally between Sarah and Benjamin. There was no legacy for the disinherited Richard but a sum of £200 was left to his trustees to cover any of his outstanding debts to them. Any money remaining was to be invested and the interest to be applied to the benefit of Richard for life and thereafter to his children.

Another trust deed of Westgate Chapel dated 1811 confirms that Benjamin had moved into St. Anne's House where he remained until he died.

Shrewd business man that he was, he could probably foresee the approaching end of the Napoleonic Wars and reasoned that this would undoubtedly mean a recession in farming. Accordingly he turned to house property as an investment and in 1812, in addition to St. Anne's House owned Nos. 39 and 49 High Street and Nos. 1 and 2 Church Street, Lewes. At a later date he also owned a house with grounds in Bond Street, Brighton.

The year before Waterloo Benjamin was certain that the approaching slump in farming would cause a fall in rents. He therefore leased to James Skinner of Finsbury Place,

London,[54] whipmaker, the Woodbrookes estate and Wickham Farm at a yearly rental of £300, reserving to himself all rights of timber, mines, hawking, fishing, hunting and foling, (possibly 'folding', i.e. the right to pen sheep). Finally in 1818 he sold the property outright for £5,500 to James Scarlett[55] K.C. of the Inner Temple. This James Scarlett was later raised to the Bench as Baron Abinger and was the last member of the English judiciary to be charged (unsuccessfully as it happened) with corruption.[56]

George Henry, the youngest son of Richard Ridge, came of age in 1835 and as executor of his father's will Benjamin had to make arrangements for the trustees to realise the estates charged to the benefit of his brother's children.

'23rd February, 1835. Affidavit[57] by Benjamin Ridge of Lewes, gent., youngest son of William Ridge, formerly of Lewes, gent.'

'Decd. that:- Deponent's mother died in December, 1811 and was buried in the burial ground of St. Michael's in Lewes.

'Richard Ridge, deponent's brother, died on 13th March, 1826, and was buried at Fletching.

'The said Richard Ridge had 12 children only, viz:- Luke, Stephen, Sarah, Richard, Ann, Caroline, Ruth, William, Lois, Maria and George Henry and one other who died soon after birth.

'George Henry was the youngest. Caroline died 23rd January 1824, unmarried and was buried at Fletching. Ruth died 11th February, 1833, unmarried and was buried at the same place.

'Ann is the wife of James Batchelor and Lois the wife of William Hollis.'

Of the original trustees only Joseph Ridge[58] of Iford remained but Benjamin, no doubt, acted as business manager in winding up the estate and the eight surviving children of his brother benefitted to the extent of about £400 each.

Benjamin died in 1849 at the age of 85, leaving everything to his two daughters. He probably tried to find husbands for them among the Iford Ridges but without success and both remained spinsters until they died, Sarah in 1866 and Mary in 1879. For nearly 300 years successive generations had striven to enrich the family and to continue the line. Now it was finished.

John Sawyer,[59] the Lewes historian, wrote of William Ridge as 'A member of a very old Sussex family connected with Lewes, *but now extinct*'. In a way this was true. The old order, which reached its peak with William Ridge, was dead but the line still continued through his disinherited and almost forgotten son, Richard.

RICHARD RIDGE OF HAMSEY
Yeoman. 1762-1826

WHATEVER HIS FAULTS, Richard settled down on a small farm at Fletching where he raised a large family. He seems to have had hopes of a reconciliation with his father for those of his children born in the 11 years between his marriage to Ann Turner and his father's death, were baptised at Westgate Meeting House in Lewes. Eventually, realising that his mother, brother and sister would have nothing to do with him, he severed all connections with Lewes and the remainder of his children were baptised at the Independent Meeting House at Ote Hall, Wivelsfield.

Curiously enough the Iford branch too was approaching its end. Sarah, the sister of William Ridge of Alciston had married a big landowner, Samuel Snashall, one of the trustees appointed by William Ridge of Lewes to manage the affairs of his son Richard. He died leaving Sarah a very wealthy woman and true to the Ridge tradition she left the bulk of her real estate in 1835 to William of Stoneham, eldest son of her brother, William of Alciston who had died three years before. William of Stoneham died unmarried and in 1848 his brother Henry inherited as principal legatee. Some idea of the accumulated family wealth may be gauged from a provision in the will of William whereby he left £10,000 to be invested on trust and the profits to be devoted to the interests of his sister Anna, married to Henry Greenhill of London. Henry Ridge never married and when he died in 1871 at the age of 79, the estate passed out of the Ridge family to the Greenhills.

Richard Ridge never had more than about 30 acres of land, part of which was copyhold and part in the ownership of his brother. The Land Tax Records for 1801 show Richard as the occupier of Burnt House with Benjamin as the owner. In the following year, however, Richard was the owner, due, in all probability to the exchange of lands at Ringmer for those at Fletching (see Codicil to the Will of William Ridge, 1802, appendix, p.73). Richard also farmed other property with the picturesque names of Plows, Land of Canaan and Marybone Fields until his death in 1826, but Burnt House remained the home of his widow until 1830.

In comparison, with their relatives at Lewes and Iford, the Ridges of Fletching were poor but the family spirit and determination to overcome the difficulties of life still remained. Knowing that he could expect nothing on the death of his father, Luke, the eldest son of Richard, migrated to Chelsea where he was joined successively by Lois, William, and George Henry. The two boys became associated with their elder brother in the cheese trade whilst Lois married William Hollis, cheesemonger of St. Pancras, Middlesex.

Stephen and Richard continued as small farmers in Fletching and in 1828 Ann married James Batchelor, schoolmaster of Fletching.

Of the four spinster sisters Caroline (died 1824) and Ruth (died 1833) were buried at Fletching, Sarah (died 1835) at Lewes and Maria (died 1891) at Gunnersbury where she was living with her nephew George Luke Ridge.

CHAPTER IX

THE INDIVIDUALISTS

UNLIKE THEIR ANCESTORS the new generation of Ridges started without inherited estates and unhampered by the tradition that the main object in life was the pursuit of wealth ultimately to be retained in the family. Instead of being part of a patriarchal community they became individualists and instead of devoting their inherited talents solely to the task of making money, they were content if they were able to live comfortably and take an intelligent interest in those things which made life interesting without necessarily being of material value.

GEORGE HENRY RIDGE OF PIMLICO, MDX.
Cheesemonger. 1814-1883

GEORGE HENRY was a youth in his teens when he left Fletching to join his eldest brother Luke, a cheesemonger of Lower Sloane Street, Chelsea. He probably worked as an apprentice until, at the age of 21, he received his share of the legacy under his grandfather's will. With this money he established his own business at 12 Grosvenor Row, Pimlico and in the following year, 1836, married Martha Jessop at St. George's Church, Hanover Square. His brother William and Selina Shanks were witnesses to the marriage. On 8 April 1838, their only child was born and was baptised Henry at St. George's in the following July. By 1841 the business was flourishing for the Census Return for that year shows that in addition to George Henry, Martha and Henry, two servants were living in the house.

Not being obsessed with the perpetual chasing of money, George Henry retired in his 60s and died at the age of 69 in Hackney. He was a true Dickensian character and his grandson remembered him as something larger than life, carrying a gold-headed cane and wearing his top hat at a rakish angle. He was a happy and contented man full of boisterous good humour.

HENRY RIDGE OF PIMLICO
Gentleman.* 1838-1890

UNAWARE of the fact that he was following the custom of his Elizabethan ancestors, George Henry apprenticed his son to a carpenter, possibly to Paradine Hodgkins, a master carpenter of Haggerston, with whom Henry was living in 1860. In August of the same year Henry Ridge married Ann Elizabeth, the 16-year-old daughter of the house, at Haggerston Parish Church.

One of Henry's friends was Joseph Degge, a young man only two years his senior but of some commercial ability since at the age of 24 he had been appointed manager of the London Office of the Royal Liver Friendly Society. On 2 February 1861, the two young men met in a coffee shop in City Road and produced the famous document written on a sheet of note-paper beginning: 'We the undersigned . . .'(Plate 14). The Royal London Life Insurance and Benefit Society had been founded.

The work of the Royal London was mainly among the weekly wage-earners and from the beginning of their partnership the founders had one over-riding principle which is still a characteristic of the Royal London to this day. Claims should not only be settled promptly but in the case of doubt the settlement should be loaded in favour of the claimant. When the first claim arose there were insufficient funds to meet it and true to their principles Henry Ridge and Joseph Degge

* The term 'gentleman' is used here in its heraldic sense, i.e. one who did not work with his hands.

The individualists

emptied their pockets on to a kitchen table doing duty as an office desk and the claim was met.

Quite openly, but completely without authority, the Royal London had appropriated to its own use the arms of the City of London and continued to use them for 70 years. In 1934 the College of Arms pointed out the unwarranted assumption eventually replacing it with the present coat of arms and the motto 'Sustenet Nos Deus'. It is a pity that the original motto 'Domine Dirige Nos' has been withdrawn — it was certainly most appropriate in the early days!

On 30 October 1861, Ann Elizabeth Ridge gave birth prematurely to twins, only one of whom survived and was baptised Charles Henry.

Altogether there were eight children of the marriage, Charles, Elizabeth, Richard, Katharine, Emily, Harold, John and Grace and when they married most of them settled in the suburbs of London. The exceptions were John, who went to New Zealand, Harold who settled in Canada and Charles Henry who eventually made his home in Brighton.

Building up the Royal London was an exacting task but Henry Ridge found time for some relaxation. His individualism manifested itself in mild eccentricities. He would return home from a tiring and worrying day at the office, shut himself in his study and play the concertina for an hour or more. Again, he would suddenly say to his wife, 'Ann, I shall be away for the next week', to which the reply would be, 'Very well, Henry'. In a few days postcards would begin to arrive from Boulogne, Rouen, Paris, Brussels, indicating that he was off on one of his solitary continental journeys.

He taught himself French using *Chardenal's First French Course* and its companion volume *Practical French Conversation*. Both these books (now in the possession of the author) are copiously annotated in Henry's writing and on a page showing money equivalents he had worked out the English prices of some additions he had made to his wardrobe in France.

'Vest 3/6d., coat 4/6d., socks 10½d., trousers 10/6d., boots 8/6d., and tie 6d.! Pasted into the back cover is an advertisement for a 12-day tour of Holland, Belgium and the Rhine. The tour also included a visit to the Battle-field of

Waterloo and cost, with first class travel and hotel accommodation, £12 12s. 0d.! From these little books Henry Ridge not only acquired a working knowledge of everyday French but would also have been able to deal with such crises as the lost pen of the gardener's aunt or the tragedy of the postillion who had been struck by lightning!

On 9 January 1890, at the age of 52, Henry Ridge, then Chairman of the Royal London, died suddenly whilst presiding at a Board Meeting at 108, Paul Street, Holywell, Shoreditch, the head office of the Society. He may have had a premonition that he was a bad insurance risk for he had no policy with his own Company.

Although not rich by the standards of modern directors, he left his widow comfortably provided for and she was able to bring up the younger members of the family without fear of penury. In later years she invested in house property, often for the benefit of one or other of her children and died at the age of 85 in full possession of her faculties and still the matriarch.

CHARLES HENRY RIDGE OF DALSTON
Gentleman. 1861-1948

CHARLES HENRY, the eldest son of Henry Ridge, was educated at a boarding school at Birchington and at the Middle Class School, Cowper Street, London. After a short period in a City office he joined his father at the Head Office of the Royal London.

He married Emily Barnes Degge, cousin of the Society's co-founder, on 7 September 1886, at St. John's Church, Hammersmith.

Shortly after his father's death, Charles Henry left the Head Office and moved to Colchester to develop the business of the Society. He acted as his own collector and it was here that his likeable nature and natural ability to make friends stood him in good stead. Returning home one night with the day's collections he was attacked by footpads. One of his attackers

The individualists

recognising him in the light of a street lamp, called out, 'Oh! It's Mr Ridge!' and the men vanished.

A few years later he moved to Brighton where he took on a vast coastal area stretching from Worthing to Eastbourne. Unknowingly he had returned to the country of his ancestors.

The first child of Charles Henry and Emily only lived for a few weeks but in 1900 a son was born and christened Dudley at Preston Old Church, Brighton.

Charles Henry inherited the mildly eccentric nature of his father and to an even greater degree his love of the French language. He was for many years a member of the local Cercle Français and attended services at the Eglise Réformée Française in Brighton. For a non-academic man his knowledge of French literature was wide and varied. He had an insatiable thirst for knowledge and although he could converse on almost any topic, he used to admit that there were three things he had never fully understood, 'Algebra, tonic sol-fa and women!' He had a great sense of humour and took enormous delight in reading aloud favourite passages from Mark Twain, the *Bab Ballads* and the *Ingoldsby Legends*. A kindly, tolerant man, he died in March 1948, in his 87th year, his last words being, 'I am very content'.

On his tombstone in the Brighton Extra-Mural Cemetery are inscribed the words, 'Sans Peur et Sans Reproche'. His wife died a few months later and lies beside him.

EPILOGUE

SINCE HISTORY DEALS with the past, this narrative rightly ends with the death of Charles Henry Ridge. His descendants, still living, should find their place in an addendum to be written some 50 years hence. However, in addition to inheriting the love of foreign languages first evident in Henry Ridge, they seem to have developed a new family trait so that if they were to be dignified by a chapter of their own it would have to be called 'THE ACADEMICS'.

As a compromise, therefore, the following notes on living members of the direct line have been added in the form of a family 'Who's Who'.

Dudley Ridge of Brighton, M.Sc., Ph.D., F.R.I.C.

Born Brighton, 31 October 1900, only son of Charles Henry Ridge. Educated Varndean School, Brighton, and University College, London. (Hallett Science Scholar.) Married Winifred Violet Lowden, 8 August 1925. One son, Alan Dudley born 2 October 1926. Lecturer in Chemistry, The Polytechnic, Regent Street, London; Head of Department of Chemistry and Biology, Barking College of Technology. 1951 H.M.I. Ministry of Education. Retired 1960. President of Tenterden and District Local History Society and Member of Sussex Archaeological Society. Author of two text-books on Chemistry and of a number of papers in scientific journals. Linguist.

Alan Dudley Ridge of Brighton. B.A.

Born Brighton, 2 October 1926, only son of Dudley Ridge. Educated Whitgift Middle School and Lancaster Royal Grammar School. Entered Honours School in History, University College, London. (New Bradshaw Scholar.) Postgraduate Diploma in Archive Administration. Assistant Archivist, London County Council; Divisional Head of Records

Epilogue

and Registry Services, Yorkshire Coalfield, National Coal Board; Archivist, McGill University, Montreal; Provincial Archivist, Province of Alberta. Married Irene Geraldine Ames, 7 March 1953. Two sons, Simon Gervase (1954) and Timothy Piers (1961). Author of a number of papers in journals of learned societies. Linguist.

Harold Laurence Ridge of Hamilton, Ontario, B.Sc., M.A.

Born Hamilton, Ontario 1937. Great-grandson of Henry Ridge of the Royal London. B.Sc. McMaster University, Dean's Honour List in Mathematics. Post Graduate student University of Toronto, M.A., 1971. Teacher of Mathematics at Burlington and at University of Toronto Schools. Co-ordinator of Mathematics Borough of York Board of Education and now Assistant Professor of Mathematics, College of Education, University of Toronto. Married Lois Maud Jackson 1960. Two children, Carolyn Lesley (1964) and Jonathan Kevin Laurence (1971). Author of a number of books on Mathematics. Musician.

REFERENCES

1. Iford Farm Deeds.
2. Sussex Record Society, xxxiv.
3. Iford Farm Deeds.
4. *Stroud's Judicial Dictionary*, 2286.
5. *The English Yeoman*, 78.
6. *The World We have Lost*, 82.
7. Ibid. 93.
8. Ibid. 32.
9. S.A.C. lxxxii, 83.
10. *Guide to Lewes*, 38.
11. Sussex Record Society, xxxiv, 17.
12. S.A.C., lxxxii, 84.
13. Sussex Record Society, xxxiv, 67.
14. Ibid. 140, 220.
15. *The English Farmhouse*.
16. *The World We have Lost*, 1.
17. Ibid. 14.
18. Ibid. 9.
19. *The English Yeoman*, 313.
20. *The World We have Lost*, 72.
21. *The English Yeoman*, 246.
22. Ibid. 251.
23. *The World We have Lost*, 13.
24. *The English Yeoman*, 263.
25. Ibid. 268.
26. Ibid. 271.
27. Ibid. 238.
28. *Contraband Cargoes*, 14.
29. Ibid. 2.
30. Ibid. 21.
31. Ibid. 27 et seq.
32. Ibid. loc. cit.
33. Ibid. 73.
34. Sussex Record Society, xxxiv, 139.
35. *The World We have Lost*, 34.
36. S.A.C., xvi, 49.
37. *Sussex Genealogies*, 92.
38. S.A.C., xxxviii, 138.
39. S.A.C., xiv, 119.
40. S.A.C., li, 12.
41. S.A.C., xxxvii, 116 et seq.
42. *The Story of an Old Meeting House*, 23.
43. Schiffner Collection, SH 165.
44. S.A.C., lxvi, 116.
45. S.N.Q., i, 210.
46. *The Countryman*, July, 1933, 372
47. *The Story of an Old Meeting House*, 137.
48. S.A.C., lxxxii, 6.
49. V.C.H., 7, 59.
50. Pelham Deeds, 338.
51. Ibid. 339.
52. Ibid. 340.
53. Schiffner Collection, SH 184.
54. Ibid. SH 166.
55. Ibid. SH 185-188.
56. *Tipping the Scales*, 170.
57. Schiffner Collection, SH 167.
58. Ibid. SH 189.
59. S.A.C., xxxvii, 116.

BIBLIOGRAPHY

Trevelyan, G.M., *English Social History* (2nd Edition, London, 1946).

Campbell, Mildred, *The English Yeoman in the Tudor and Early Stuart Age* (English Edition, London, 1967).

Laslett, Peter, *The World We have Lost* (London, 1965).

Barley, M.W., *The English Farmhouse and Cottage* (London, 1961).

Williams, Neville, *Contraband Cargoes* (London, 1959).

Victoria County History of England (V.C.H.) (London, 1940).

Cecil, Henry, *Tipping the Scales* (London, 1964).

Book of John Rowe (Sussex Record Society, xxxiv, 1928).

Sawyer, John, *Guide to Lewes* (Ringmer, 1899).

Horsfield, T.W., *History and Antiquities of Lewes and its Vicinity* (Lewes, 1824, 1827).

Stroud's Judicial Dictionary (2nd Edition, London, 1903).

Berry, William, *Sussex Pedigrees* (London, 1830).

Comber, John, *Sussex Genealogies* (Cambridge, 1933).

Connell, J.M., *The Story of an Old Meeting House* (2nd Edition, London, 1935).

Sussex Archaeological Collections. (S.A.C.)

Sussex Notes and Queries (S.N.Q.)

Iford Farm Deeds (unclassified at the time of inspection (1967)). East Sussex Record Office, Lewes.

Pelham Deeds. Sussex Archaeological Society.

Schiffner Collection. Sussex Archaeological Trust.

Deeds of Westgate Chapel. A.J. Roper (Private communication).

Wills, Post Mortem Inventories, Tithe Maps, Land Tax Records &c. East Sussex Record Office, Lewes.

The Town Books. Municipal Borough of Lewes.

APPENDIX

WILL OF JOHN RIDGE OF OVINGDEAN   Died 1558

In the name of god amen the vj day of July in ye yeare of our lord god 1558 I John Rige husbandman of the parishe of Ovynden . . . In the County of sussex being of perfet memorye but syke In body do orden and make my last will and testament in manner and form followyng fyrst and principall I geve and bequethe my Soule unto Almyghty god my maker redemer and only savyor by whom my assured trust is to be savyd and my body I bequeth to be buryed in the Churcheyard groundes to the whiche Church I geve vj s. viijd. that I have payd for an . . .
Item I geve to the mother Church of the . . .
Item I geve and bequethe to thomas my son £x of good lawful mony of England to be payd to him at the day of his marrege Item I geve to agnes my dowghter £x of good and lawful mony of England to be payd to her at the day of her marrege Item I geve to tompson my dowghter £x of good and lawfull mony of England to be payd to her at the day of her marrege also I geve to every of them a cow and a haffer and iij . . . sheppe to be delivered at the annunciation of ye blyssed lady next after the marrages at the discretion of my executors provyded alway that yf any of them dye after they by marryed then his or her parte or portion afore wylled so devysed shall remayn and be to the executors of this my last will and testament. Item I geve to Richard pullyngton my kynsman a haffer of ij yeres old and to Richard blunden my friend an ewe and a lambe to be delivered to them owt of hand
    The residew of my goods moveable and unmoveable my detts payd I geve and bequethe to Agnes my wyfe and John my son whom I make and orden my only executores. In witnes hereof I have caused these to be writtyn ye day and yere above mentioned these being my overseares hugh

okyenden and John guymer gyvyng to every of them vj^s viij^d and these being my witnesses Item I geve to the poore ... vj^s viij^d to be distributed for ... to them at my buryall and at my mether chyrch Witness hereof John Okenden Philip guymer and others

Summa , ... iiij^{xx} xv^{li} vj^s xj^d

WILL OF AGNES RIDGE OF OVINGDEAN Died 1559

In the name of God amen. The last day of November in the yere of our Lord God 1559 I Agnes Rydge wydowe of Ovyngden in the County of Sussex beyng of good and perfyt Remembraunce thanks be to Allmyghty god byt sycke in bodye do ordeyn and make this my present testament and last wyll in manner and forme following. fyrst and princypally I commytte and bequethe my Soulle to Allmyghtye god my maker to Jesu Christ my only redemer and savyor by whom only my assured hope ys to be savyed and my body to be buryed in the churche yeard of Ovyngden by my husband to the which church I geve xijd to the reparacons of the sayd churche Item to the churche of Chichester I geve xijd Item I geve to Agnes my dowghter one cowe one quarter of wheat one quarter of malte one blankett ye worst of my too best gownes my redd kyrtell my petycote that ys at makyng a good kerchiffe and my best vayll Item I geve to Tomsen my dowghter one cowe one quarter of wheat one quarter of mault my best gowne, my sylver taches a worsted kyrtell my petycote that I weare the holydayes a kerchef that ys unmade and a vaylle Item I geve to Thomas my sonne a cowe a quarter of wheat a quarter of mault and a baskett to be delyvered to him at thage of xx^{ti} yeres And I wyll that yf any of them dye before they be payd that the partes of him or her beyng dead shalbe devyded amongest them that be a lyve Item I geve to Agnes my dowghter in hamshere one cowe Item I geve to my sonne bottyng and to my dowghter his wyfe £iiij of lawfull monye of England Item I wyll that my dowghter botting shall have my best kerchief Item I geve to Rychard pollington one ewe shepe

The Resydewe of all my goods I geve to John my sonne whom I make my executor desiring Mr Goring to be my overseer these being witnesses Ryc. Pollyngt. and John Guymar and others.

WILL OF STEPHEN (I) RIDGE SENIOR Died 1637/8

In the Name of God amen The seven and twentieth day of March in the yeare of our Lord God one thousand six hundred thirty and seven I Stephen Ridge Senior of Iford in the County of Sussex Yeoman being weak of body but of good and perfecte memory God bee praysed, doe make and ordayne this my last will and Testament whereby after the bequeathing of My Soule into the Hands of Almighty God my Creator, Redeemer and Sanctifier and my body to the earth my worldly goods I thus dispose Imprimis I give unto the poore of the parrish of Iford twenty shillings to bee given and distributed among them by myne Executor on the day of my buriall Item I give and bequeath unto my sonne in Lawe James Harman that Lease which I gave of the Farme Boldee lying in Barcombe parrish Item I give and bequeath unto my daughter Alice the wife of the said James Harman the some of twenty pounds of lawfull money of England, to bee payd unto her within an yeare next after my decease Item I give unto Anne Harman my grandchilde the some of Ten pounds of lawfull money of England to bee payd unto her when she shall accomplish the age of one and Twenty yeares Item I give unto Jane Harman my grandchilde Ten Pounds of lawfull money of England to bee payd unto her when she shall accomplishe the age of one and Twenty yeares Item I give unto Emline Backshell my grandchilde the like some of Ten Pounds of lawfull money of England to bee payd unto her when shee shall accomplishe the age of one and Twenty yeares Item I give unto Joane Backshell my grandchilde the some of Ten Pounds of lawfull money of England to be payd unto her when shee shall accomplishe the age of one and Twenty yeares Item I give unto Nicholas Backshell my grandchilde the some of Ten Pounds of lawfull money of England to bee payd unto him when hee shall accomplish the age of one and Twenty yeares Item I give unto my grandchilde Thomas Ridge the sonne of Thomas Ridge late deceased the some of Ten Pounds of lawfull money of England to be payd unto him when he shall accomplishe the age of one and Twenty yeares Item I give unto Mary Ridge my grandchilde the daughter of the foresayd Thomas Ridge the some of Ten pounds of lawfull money of England to bee payd unto her when she shall accomplishe the age of one and twenty yeares Item I give and bequeathe unto Mary Frend my grandchilde the some of Ten Pounds of lawfull money to bee payd unto her when she shall accomplishe the age of one and Twenty yeares Item I give unto my grandchild Stephen Ridge the sonne of Stephen Ridge the some of Ten Pounds of lawfull money of England to bee payd unto him when he shall accomplishe the age of one and Twenty yeares Item I give unto my grandchild Thomas Ridge the sonne of Stephen Ridge the some of Ten Pounds of lawfull money to bee payd unto him when he shall accomplishe the age of one and Twenty yeares Item I give unto Agnes Ridge my grandchilde the daughter of Stephen Ridge the some of Ten Pounds of lawfull money of England to be payd unto her when she shall accomplishe the age of one and Twenty yeares Item I give unto my grandchild John Ridge the sonne of Stephen Ridge the some of Ten Pounds of lawfull money of England to bee payd unto him when hee shall accomplishe the age of one and Twenty yeares Item I give unto my grandchild Richard Ridge the sonne of Stephen Ridge the some of Ten Pounds of lawfull money of England to bee payd unto him when hee shall accomplish the age of one and Twenty yeares Item I give and bequeathe to every one of my godchildren that shall be living at the day of my decease the some of two shillings and six pence a peece of lawfull money of England to be delivered and payd unto them or unto theire Parents for them and for theire use within one moneth next after my decease Item I will that all such debts and dues as shalbe owing unto any manner of person whatsoever of mee of Right and Consciense be well and truly contented satisfied and payd by myne Executor hereafter named. All

Appendix

the rest of my goods and chattels whatsoever not given and bequeathed my debts being payd and my funerall expensses being discharged I give and bequeath unto my sonne Stephen Ridge whome I doe make and ordayne my sole Executor of this my last will and Testament and doe give and appointe unto him the Guardianship and tuition of the foresaid Thomas Ridge sonne of Thomas Ridge late deceased if so bee that the Lawes will so permitt and suffer it and I do request my welbeloved freinde Mr John Aylwin of Lewes gent and Alexander Alchorne of Firle to bee overseers of the performance of this my last Will and Testament unto whome I do give the some of Forty shillings apeece for theire paynes and as a small token of my love and I doe hereby revoake and dissnull all former Wills by mee made In witness whereof I have unto this my present will written uppon three sheets of paper subscribed and fixed my seale at the topp the day and yeare above written   Stephen Ridge his marke

Signed sealed and acknowledged in the presence of

                John Newland his marke
                Margaret Rogers
                Thomas Rogers

ABSTRACT OF WILL OF STEPHEN RIDGE OF LEWES
Yeoman Died 1714

Will of Stephen Ridge of Lewes, Yeoman . . . perfect in mind and memory . . . 12th November in the tenth year of the reign of our Sovereign Lady Anne of Great Britain, France and Ireland, Queen, Fid. Def. A.D. 1711.

To the poor of the congregation of Lewes of which I am a member 15/-.

To my son Stephen £50.

To daughters Ann and Sarah £100 each at age 27.

To my grandsons John Crawley and William Crawley and to grand daughters Sarah Crawley and Ann Crawley £10 each at 21.

To grand daughter Mary Crawley at 21 or day of marriage £?

To son-in-law John Crawley £20.

To my loving wife Joan to use of all my household stuffe and goods now in my dwelling house in St. Mary Lane in Lewes for her natural life. Also to my said wife for the duration of her natural life an annual sum of £30.

Also I give to my daughter Elizabeth in case she should happen to survive my said wife and as long as she shall continue sole and unmarried a yearly sum of £14.

Concerning my copyhold tenement, barne, meadow, pasture, common pasture and arable lands with appurtenances lying in the said Parish of Iford in the south part of the common lands there holden of the Manors of Northesium and Iford or one of them and which I have formerly surrendered to the use of my will I give to my son Richard Ridge.

To Stephen Ridge all my lands called Woodbrooks for and during for a term of 99 years if he shall so long live and after the determination of that estate I devise the same to my son Richard Ridge upon trust to support the contingent remainders. After the decease of Stephen Ridge to the heirs male and in default to son Richard, his heirs and assigns for ever paying to the daughter of the said Stephen Ridge if he shall happen to leave but one the sum of £300. Should there be more than one daughter £600 share and share alike.

The rest of my personal estate to son Richard who is executor.

Witnesses Thos. Isted.
Richard Godley
Mary Stone

ABSTRACT OF WILL OF RICHARD RIDGE OF LEWES
Gent. Died 1755

11th March 1754
Legacies to:—

Wife Ann Ridge (Packham) an annuity of £24 for life and all

Appendix

the house hold goods.
Sister Sarah Pope of Southover, widow, an annuity of £6 for life.
Grand-daughter Elizabeth Ridge, only daughter of son John Ridge, £100.
Grandson Stephen Weller, only child of daughter Ann, decd. late wife of Cruttenden Weller, £100.
Residual legatee and executor eldest son William Ridge. Declaration that lease of Upper Stoneham Farm in which testator joined belongs to son William.
Devise to said eldest son William of the copyhold barn called the Lower Barn with orchard and lands called Wickham and Rowley in the parish of St. John-sub-Castro in the occupation of Samuel Ridge and held of the Manor of Allington, and also 2 parcels of copyhold land called Pole Roofes, land containing 8 acres with sheep leazes in Hamsey in the occupation of the said Samuel Ridge and held of the Manor of Hamsey.
To youngest son John Ridge, 2 parcels of copyhold land of new assert containing 20 acres called Hartlings Field and Cockles, otherwise Scrub Hall and a piece of new assert called Sessinghams containing 3a. 3r. all in the Borough of Peckham in Framfield, holden of the Manor of Framfield.

WILL OF WILLIAM RIDGE OF LEWES Gent. Died 1802

Will of William Ridge, gent., of the Parish of St. Peter and St. Mary Westout in Lewes.
   Sworn that goods, chattles and credits do not exceed £5000.
   All freehold and tenement left to Sarah Ridge and after her death to youngest son Benjamin, his heirs and assigns,
                      Woodbrooks, Chailey;
                      Upper Wickham Farm;
                      Lower Wickham and Rowley.
   To wife, household goods, plate, linen, china, library of books, wood, coal, garden tools, wearing apparel absolutely.

An annuity of £50 out of estates Woodbrooks etc., all in tenure and occupation of Benjamin Ridge. The annuity to be paid clear of all taxes etc. If the annuity or rent charge be unpaid for 21 days the wife may enter and distrain.

£1200 to wife Sarah to be paid by son Benjamin out of rent and personal estate hereinafter given to him.

To daughter Sarah, wife of William Ridge of Alciston, legacy of £700 to be paid by Benjamin out of real and personal estate.

I give and devise to my son-in-law, William, friends Saml. Snashall of Lewes and Joseph Ridge of Iford, gent. all that my freehold messuage or tenement farm land and hereditaments commonly called Grammar Staples situate near Clay Hill in the Parish of Ringmer late in the tenure and occupation of John Davey the younger and now of my son Benjamin with all the timber and other rights. To hold the same unto the use of the said William Ridge, Samuel Snashall and Joseph Ridge upon trust that the said William Ridge, Samuel Snashall and Joseph Ridge shall receive and take the rents and profits of the last mentioned messuage lands etc for and during the natural lives of my son Richard Ridge and Ann his wife and the life of the longest liver of them and from thereafter until the youngest child of Richard lawfully gotten shall attain the age of 21 years and shall yearly during the natural life of Richard pay unto him the said rents and profits or such part of them as they shall think proper shall do pay and apply the residue thereof (if any) towards the support and maintenance of the wife and children of my said son Richard. After the decease of my said son Richard if the said Ann be then living pay unto her the sum of £14 per annum clear of taxes and deductions and the residue of the said rents to the maintenance or otherwise of the said children of Richard. On the decease or second marriage of Ann the whole of the said rents and profits to the maintenace and education or otherwise for the equal benefit and advantage of all the said children of Richard until the youngest shall attain the age of 21 years.

Further trust after the death of both Richard and Ann or her second marriage when the youngest of the said children shall attain the age of 21 years then the said William Ridge,

Appendix

Samuel Snashall and Joseph Ridge or the survivors shall sell and dispose of my said farmlands in Ringmer to the best purchaser and upon further trust pay and divide the said purchase money between the children of the said Richard lawfully begotten then living (children of deceased children to inherit). Failing any lawful claimants whole of the property to Benjamin his heirs etc absolutely.

Also I give and bequeath unto the said William Ridge, Samuel Snashall and Joseph Ridge one annuity and rent charge of £68 for the term of the natural life of my son Richard and until his youngest child shall attain the age of 21 chargeable upon Woodbrooks, Upper Wickham, Lower Wickham and Rowleys. Upon trust that the said William Ridge, Samuel Snashall and Joseph Ridge shall apply the said annuity of £68 for the benefit of my son Richard, wife, children etc. When the annuity ceases I give and bequeath to William Ridge, Samuel Snashall and Joseph Ridge the sum of £1700 charged upon and to be paid to them by my son Benjamin Ridge out of my aforesaid farms etc. in the parishes of Chailey and St. John under the Castle, Lewes. The trustees to divide the £1700 between the children of Richard (children to inherit). The trustees are empowered either in the lifetime of Richard or after his decease to advance part of the said principal sum of £1700 of the share of such child or children would become entitled to on attaining 21 years for putting him or her out to apprentice or otherwise. The money to be raised by Benjamin on giving him six months notice. Interest at 4 per cent. per annum to be deducted from the annuity of £68.

Provided if Richard shall sell or assign his right or interest in the product of the said lands of Ringmer or the said annuity of £68 or do anything to encomber them then the trustees from thenceforth shall apply the whole of the rents, profits and annuity for the benefit of the said children of the said Richard and his wife the same as if he was dead. The trustees shall think the most for the benefit of his family it being my intention that the same shall not be subject to debts, engagements or control by my said son Richard.

I give and devise to my son Benjamin — freehold, leasehold and copyhold — Woodbrookes, Upper Wickham, Lower Wickham and Rowleys subject to the annuity of £50 to my wife and £68 to the trustees.

Permission to Benjamin to sell property which will be released from the payments of the said annuities provided Benjamin purchases other lands of sufficient value (approved by the trustees) and they shall be charged with the said annuities. Also to Benjamin copyhold lands etc. in the parish of Barcombe in the occupation of Edward Hollingdale. All other lands, tenements etc. whatsoever to the use of my said son Benjamin Ridge, his heirs and assigns for ever. All my mortgages, bonds, bills, notes, ready money and securities for money, Title Deeds and writings and all other personal estate and effects to Benjamin. Lastly I nominate Benjamin my sole executor.

Date of Will 16th September, 1797

                      Witnesses. William Cooper of Lewes
                              Attorney at Law.
                              Thomas Hill
                              P. Stone   Clerks

CODICIL

Freehold of farm and lands Grammer Staples, Ringmer, in occupation of Benjamin Ridge to hold to the use of William Ridge, Samuel Snashall and Joseph Ridge on trust for the benefit of my son Richard, his wife and children. Whereas my son Benjamin is now seized of several pieces of copyhold land — 20 acres called Burnt House purchased of James Phelp Esq., now in the occupation of my said sons Benjamin and Richard. Benjamin has also purchased several other pieces of copyhold land — 18 acres in the Parish of Fletching. Whereas the said messuage and land — more convenient to be used by my son Richard than the said lands Grammer Staples devised by my said will in trust for the benefit of Richard. Benjamin has agreed the said lands in Fletching be surrended in trust for the benefit of Richard on condition my giving to Benjamin the said lands in Ringmer. I hereby revoke etc. — such parts of my will — as relate to the devise — Grammer Staples.

In witness whereof set my hand and seal
11th Day of April in the year of our Lord 1802.

                The mark X and seal William Ridge
Witnesses.   Benjamin Ridge, Brother to the Testator's w
                William Cooper, Attorney.
                Thomas Hill.

Sworn goods, chattels and credits not more than £1000

POST MORTEM INVENTORY
JOHN RIDGE OF IFORD. Died 1612

A true and perfect Inventoire of all singular Goodes and Chattells of JOHN A'RIDGE of Iford in the Countie of Sussex, deceased, prised by Thomas Geere and Rd. Dumbrell, the seventh daie of September, 1612.

INVENTORIE

Imprimis his weareing apparrell	v lb.		
Item his girdle purse and money	xl lb.		
Item one feather bedd, two feather bolstars, ij pillowes, ij blanckette, ij coverlette	iij lb.		
Item paire sheets ij paire of pillocoats ij tableclothes		l s.	
Item three chestes		x s.	
Item one pike and corslett furnished		x s.	
Item one brasse pott		v s.	
Item one tabud and sword		iij s.	iiij d.
Item five small beaste	vi lb.		
Item eight score and vij sheep	xlj lb.	x s.	
Item three quarters of wheate	iij lb.	xij s.	
Item two steeres of iij yeares grouth	v lb.		
Item two twelvemonthings		xxx s.	
Item three weyners		xx s.	
Item omitted next to the wheate six quarters of barley	iiij lb.	xij s.	
Item two steeres of ij yeares grouth	iiij lb.		
Item eight oxen	xxx lb.		
Item six keene and a bull	xiij lb.		
Item cxxx Ewes, Weathers and Rams	xxxj lb.		
Item two horssebeaste	v lb.		
Item eight quarters of wheate	x lb.	xiij s.	iiij d.

Item xviij quarters of barley	xij lb.
Item xxtie bushels of beans	xl s.
Item vj bushells of pease	xij s.
Item three bushells of tares	v s.
Item one bushell and ½ of hempseed	iiij s.
Item one weyne, a plough, one paire of plow wheels, one share, ij coulters, v yokes, iiij tyces and ij chapes	xl s.
Item two paires of wayne wheles, ij caert, ij paire of dills, xij whippens	iij lb.
Item xx wattells	x s.
Item wood and coale	v lb.
Item x hogges of bacon and live hogges	v lb.
Item iiij bedstedds, one feather bedd, vij feather bolstars, vj covlettes and ix blanckettes	vj lb.
Item viij paire sheetes, vij cord clothes, iiij table napkins and two walletts	xxx s.
Item ij chestes and vj sackes	xvj s.
Item x pewter platters, iij pewter saucers	x s.
Item vij pertes of brass, a furnace	xl s.
Item a counter, a table, ij formes	v s.
Item ij yron potts, j pothoke, ij potthangers	x s.
Item xxv tubbs & wodden vessells	xl s.
Item xiij trugges & booles and v wodden platters	xx s.
Item ij axes and iij wedges	ij s.
Item vj candlesticks & iij salt cellers	v s.
Item in Desperate Deste	c.iiij lb.

Summa totlis (sic.)
vj.c lv lb. xiij s. viij d.

Appendix

POST MORTEM INVENTORY
JOHN RIDGE OF IFORD. Died 1710

A true and perfect Inventory of all and singular the Goods, Chattels and C . . . (?) of JOHN RIDGE late of Iford in the County of Sussex, Yeoman, deceased. Taken and appraized the Twenty third Day of June Anno Dmi 1710 by those whose names are subscribed, as follows vis.

Imprimis His wearing apparrell and money in his purse	£10.00.00
In the Kitchen. Item Jack, one spitt, one dripping pann, one clock, one warming pann, four dishes of pewter, Six plates and one chees plate.	03.10.06
In the Brewhouse. Item two ffurnaces, five barrells, four tubbs, one kooler, one Charne and one Chees-press	06.10.00
In the Milkhouse. Item three milk loads, four Truggs, two Koolers, four Barrells and three Powdering Tubbs.	02.05.00
In the Back-Kitchen. Item one pair of Andirons, and Tongs, two pair of Pothangers, two porridge pots, one iron Kettle, two Spitts, one Dripping pann and three Skilletts.	02.11.00
In the Back Chamber. Item one ole Bedd and Stoole and all belonging to him.	01.00.00
In the Backhouse. Item one Still, one Roole, two Wheels, one Tubb and one Kooler.	00.10.00
In the Kitchen Chamber. Item one Bedd and Stoole, Curtains, Vallence and Coverlett and all belonging to him, eight pair of Sheets, twelve Napkins, five Table cloths and one Chest.	10.07.06
Item one Silver Salt Celler (?) and four Silver Spoons.	01.15.06
Item Sixteen Bushells of Wheat	04.10.00
Item for Wooll	20.00.00
Stock without doors. Item nine working Oxen, two three-yearling Steers, and three twelve-monthings.	110.10.00

Item two Calves, five milch Cows, three Horses,
five Hoggs, 125 weather Sheep, 125 Ewes and
86 Lambs and Ramms.   100.05.00

Corn on the Ground. Item twenty one acres of
Wheat, 38 acres of Barley and sixteen Acres of
Grass, Tares and Oats.   119.05.00

Husbandry Tackling. Item one waggon, one Coart,
three Barrows, two Watering troughs, three
Chains and five Yokes.   07.17.00

Item Money at Interest and other Debts   50.00.00

Item for Things unseen and forgott   01.00.00

Sume Totall   £451.16.06

Thomas Ade
Stephen Ade   Appraizers
John Ridge   1710

POST MORTEM INVENTORY
STEPHEN RIDGE OF LEWES. Died 1714

A true and perfect inventory of all and singular the goods and chattells of Stephen Ridge of the Parish of St. John's in Lewes late decd. as it was taken and apprized on the 3rd January, 1714 by us whose names are underwritten.

Imprimis His wearing apparrell and money in
purse   £05.00.00

In the kitchen. Item One dresser two tables, one
clock and case, Nine chayres, two stools, ten
and twenty pewter plates and jack and spitt,
two pairs of andirons, two warming panns and
some other things not mentioned.   05.00.00

In the parlour. Item one table and five chayres   00.10.00
Item in the wood house wood and faggotts.   02.10.00

In the Buttery. Item one ffrying pann, one
chest and powdering tubb, one Spinning wheell,
yarn, winders and shelves.   01.01.06

Appendix

In the Celler. Item Two stolloges, two tubbs and six barrells.	01.00.06
In the Brewhouse. Item one ffornard, three tubbs, three ?, three porridge potts, two brass kettles and pewter and brass.	00.13.00
In the kitchen chamber. Item one cot and bedstead and all belonging thereto, nine chayres, one joyned chest and close stooll, one small table and a glass cage.	04.10.00
In the Brewhouse chamber. Item two bedds and bedsteads and all belonging thereto, two chayres and sideboard, one chest of drawers, one chest and one trunk and a looking glass.	04.02.06
In the buttery chamber. Item two bedds and bedsteads and all belonging thereto, one chest and a looking glass and linnen.	15.03.06
Item for rent and money upon Bill.	15.00.00
Item Things unseen and forgotten.	00.05.00
Totall	£56.16.00

J. Ollive.   Jos. Attersoll.

POST MORTEM INVENTORY
JOHN RIDGE OF CHAILEY. Died 1733

A full and true account of the money and goods of John Ridge, lately deceased.

Money in pocket and wearing apparrel	£3. 0. 0
A fflock bed and all belonging to it	15. 0
Two chests and a cupboard	4. 6
And other things unseen and forgotten	1. 0
	£4. 0. 6

Taken by. us   William Wolf
              Thomas Hoad

POST MORTEM INVENTORY
STEPHEN RIDGE OF CHAILEY. Died 1736

Imprimis his wearing apparrell & money in purse	£5. 0. 0
Item in the kitchen, 1 clock and jack, 1 table, forms and warming-pan, 2 porridge pots and two pairs pothooks, 4 chairs, 1 ... & other small things	5.10. 6
Item in the brewhouse, 1 furnace, 1 brewfate, 4 tubbs, 4 hookers, 1 cheese-press and other small things	4. 3. 0
Item in the best drink buttery, 1 powdring tubbe, small barrells and other small things	10. 0
Item in the milk house, 1 barn stool	10. 0
Item in the small drink buttery, 4 small barrells, 2 powdring tubbes, 3 sives and some small things	15. 0
Item in the kitchen chamber, 1 feather bed and appurtenances, 1 chest of drawers, 2 chests and some other things	4.14. 0
Item in the closet, 1 hose stool, 4 chests, 11 pair of sheets, 1 doz. of napkins, 7 tablecloathes	4.16. 0
Item in one other closet, 10 dishes of pewter, 1 doz. of plates, 6 trenchers	1. 2. 6
Item in the brewhouse chamber, 1 feather bed and appurtenances, 1 small table, 2 pair andirons, 3 chaires	5.10. 0
Item in the little chamber and closet, one bed, two milk loads, two milk koolers, one tray and one churn	9.18. 0
Item in the garrett, one old bed, one brass kettle, one tubb, one kooler, ten sacks, three leather baggs, one sheaf oats and some other things	5. 3. 0
Item rick of hay, two steers and one ox, seven cows and seven calves, two horses, 2 yearling steers and 4 twelve-monthing steers	59. 5. 0
Item four troggs	2. 0. 0
Item two wagons, two carts, three harrows, one plow and one strick plow	14.15. 0

Appendix

Item three yokes and five chains, one mathook,
one pick, two saddles   2. 8. 0
Item three horse harness, one bushell, two sives,
one pair winners, one iron barr, six prongs, one
spade, two wantys   1.17. 0
Item One roode wheat on ye ground   7. 0. 0
Item ye oats on ye ground some five quarters
and plowing and sowing   6. 0. 0
Item ye faggotts in ye stack and about ye ground   2.10. 0
Item one sledge and two wedges   7. 0
Item lost, unseen and forgotten   10. 0

      Sum totall £138. 5. 0

DEED OF CONVEYANCE OF WOODBROOKES FARM
1661

TO ALL CHRISTIAN PEOPLE to whom this present writing shall come Stephen Aridge the elder of Iford in the County of Sussex yeoman sendeth greeting in our Lord God everlasting Know ye that the said Stephen Aridge for the naturall love and affecion which he beareth unto Stephen Aridge the younger eldest sonne of Stephen Aridge the elder and for diverse other good consideracions him hereunto especially making HATH given granted infeoffed and confirmed and by these presents doth give grant infeoff and confirm unto the said Stephen Aridge the younger his heirs and assigns for ever ALL those messuages and tenements barns buildings garden and orchards lands and hereditaments whatsoever with the appurtenances conteyning by estimacion three score and ten acres be it more or less commonly called or known by the name of Woodbrookes or by what other name or names the same or any part thereof be called or knowne situate lying and being together in Chailey in the said County of Sussex and bounding to the King's Highway leading from Lewes towards the church of Chailey aforesaid towards the east To the River running from Chiltington mill towards Barcombe south To the lands of Anne Middleton widow sometyme Faukners and to the lands late of John Baily Sometyme Woods on the west and north And also the reversion and reversions of all and singular the premises Together with all and singular other the lands Tenements and Hereditaments whatsoever of the Said Stephen Aridge the elder in Chailey aforesaid And also the moyety or halfe part of all and all manner of Tithes as well great as small coming growing and renning or which hereafter shall come grow and renne of in and upon all and every or any the lands Tenements and hereditaments aforesaid sometymes parcell of the portion of Tithes etc borne also Wenchorne Together with all deeds charters evidences writings and myniments touching or concerning the premisses or any part thereof **TO HAVE AND**

Appendix

TO HOLD all and every the aforesaid messuages barnes buildings land tenements hereditaments Tithes portions and premisses and every part and parcell thereof with all their and every of their appurtenances unto the said Stephen Aridge the younger his heirs and assigns to the onely use and behoofe of the said Stephen Aridge the younger his heirs and assigns for ever IN WITNESS whereof the said Stephen Aridge the elder hath hereunto set his hand and Seale the Two and Twentieth day of July in the thirteenth yeare [dated from the death of Charles I, 1649] of the raigne of our Soveraigne Lord Charles the Second by the grace of God of England Scotland France and Ireland King Defender of the Faithe etc 1661.

DORSE

Sealed and delivered and possession and seizin of the messuages lands and premisses within mentioned was had taken and delivered

ARMORIAL BEARINGS OF THE RIDGE FAMILY

William Berry in *Sussex Pedigrees,* published in 1830, gives the pedigree of the Chichester branch of the family, starting with John Ridge of Ovingdean, together with arms blazoned as follows:

Arms: *Gules, a cross engrailed, argent. In the first quarter a trefoil, slipped, vert.* Crest: *A peacock in his pride, argent.*

The tincture of the trefoil is suspect as it is against all the rules of armory to blazon *vert* on *gules* but Berry, formerly a clerk employed in the College of Arms, was no genealogist and his works contain numerous errors of this nature. In making his collections of County Pedigrees he appears to have copied some of the Coats of Arms from the Heraldic Visitations and from the Harleian Manuscripts in the British Museum, whilst the remainder were obtained by writing to county families for their pedigrees and armorial bearings. Burke's *Genealogical Armory,* 1884, is heraldically correct in its blazon for Ridge (Chichester, Co. Sussex) — Arms: *Gules, A cross engrailed, argent; In the dexter chief quarter a trefoil slipped, or.* Crest: *A peacock in his pride, argent.*

From Berry's restriction of armorial bearings to the Chichester family, it would appear that neither the direct nor the Iford branch claimed to be armigerous although Luke Ridge, a cousin of Henry Ridge, used the arms on a book plate together with the motto 'Dum Vivimus Vivamus' — (While we live let us live). It is of interest to note that in volume I of *The Book of Family Crests,* Washburn, 1882, this motto is ascribed to the famous Nonconformist divine, Dr. Doddridge, (see p.33) and is a Latin transcription of the first line of one of his hymns.

> 'Live while you live, an epicure would say,
> And snatch the pleasures of the present day;
> Live while you live, the sacred preacher cries
> And give to God each moment as it flies,
> Lord! In Thy view let both united be!
> I live in pleasure when I live in Thee!'

Appendix

It is likely that Luke Ridge saw the arms in Berry's *Sussex Pedigrees* and added the motto as a connecting link with his own branch of the family.

The Chichester Ridges had married into the wealthy Lacey family and later acquired greater prosperity and county status by service in the East India Company. It seemed likely, therefore, that the armorial bearings would date from about the middle of the 18th century. Enquiry at the College of Arms, however, showed that although there were three registered pedigrees, all starting from John Ridge of Ovingdean, no grant of arms was made until 10 December 1935, when Cecil Harold Ridge of the Chichester line, received Letters Patent rehearsing the fact that the Arms *Gules, a cross engrailed, argent, in the first quarter a trefoil slipped, or;* together with the Crest *A peacock in his pride, argent,* were long used by his paternal ancestors but do not appear to have been recorded in the College of Arms. The grant confirms the Arms but makes a difference in the Crest: *On a rock proper, a peacock in his pride, argent, collared or.* Identical arms were granted in 1950 to Robert Leslie Ridge of Enfield, a collateral of Cecil Harold Ridge.

The last Heraldic Visitation to record the arms of county families was in 1686 and it is not surprising therefore, that a large number of families becoming wealthy in the 18th century, assumed arms without having them recorded at the College of Arms.

The original designer of the arms assumed by the Chichester branch must have had some knowledge of local history and its connection with the family. In the 15th century the Manor of Northease-cum-Iford was held by the Dalynrigges whose arms were *Argent, a cross engrailed gules,* (counter-changed for Ridge), whilst the crest, *A peacock in his pride, argent,* was borrowed from the Pelhams of Lewes and Laughton!

DIRECT DESCENT

John Ridge of Ovingdean, = Agnes Pollington
Husbandman. b. 1506? d. 1558. | d. 1559

```
            Agnes = ... Botting    Tompson    John Ridge of Iford, = Joane ...    Thomas
                                              Yeoman. b. 1533? d. 1612 | d.1609
```

```
George    Richard    Stephen Ridge of Iford,  = Margaret ...         Mary = Richard Dumbrill
                     Yeoman. b. 1560? d. 1638 | d. 1627
```

```
John  Thomas  George  (1) Mary Howell = Stephen Ridge of Iford, = Jane Alchorne (2)   Alice   Dionese   Johanna
              of Chinting. d. 1625 |   Yeoman. b. 1590?    | m. 1625. d. 1660
                                       d.1664
```

```
Thomas of the Cliffe, = Elizabeth   John   Egbert   Richard   Stephen Ridge of Westmeston, = Joan Marchant   William = (1) Hannah   Anne   Agnes   Mary
Draper. 1625-1678   | Palmer                                 Yeoman. b. 1626 d. 1714   | of Ditchling.           (2) Mary
                                                                                        m. 1670
```

SOUTHOVER BRANCH   **CHICHESTER BRANCH**
                                                                                                                                    FORD BRANCH

```
Stephen of Chailey = (1) Mary   John   Thomas   Mary   Richard Ridge of S. Malling, = Anne Packham of     Joan   Elizabeth   Jane   Anne   Sarah
                     (2) Elizabeth                     Gentleman. b.1681 d. 1755  | Framfield, b. 1681
                     2 Daughters                                                   m. 1708 d. 1764
```

```
(1) Elizabeth = John Ridge of         = (2) Anne   Thomas   William Ridge of Lewes, = Sarah Ridge of Iford   Jane   Anne   Mary = Rev. Ebenezer Johnston
    d. 1739    Stoneham, Gentleman. b.1710  d.1773            Gentleman. b.1709 d. 1802 | b. 1730 m. 1757 d. 1811
               d.1778
```

```
Benjamin Ridge of Chailey, = Sarah Palmer    Luke         Richard Ridge of Hamsey, = Anne Turner of           Sarah = William Ridge
Gentleman. b. 1764 d.1849   m. 1795         ob. inf.     Yeoman. b. 1761 d. 1826   Fletching. m. 1791                of Alciston
                            2 daughters     2 years                                                                                    a child
                                                                                                                                       ob. inf.
                                                                                                                                       19 days.

Luke  Stephen  William  Richard  Sarah   George Hy. Ridge of Pimlico, Mdx. = Martha Jessop    Anne   Caroline   Ruth    Lois   Maria   Grace
                                         Cheesemonger. b. 1814 d. 1883    m. 1836

                                                    Henry Ridge of Pimlico, Mdx. = Anne Elizabeth Hodgkins
                                                    Gentleman. b. 1838 d. 1890    m. 1860 d. 1929

Richard    Harold Ridge of Dalston. = Louisa Winder    John   Charles Hy. Ridge of Dalston, = Emily Barnes Degge    Elizabeth   Katherine   Emily
           (To Canada) d. 1949                                Gentleman. b. 1861 d. 1948    m. 1886 d. 1948

Harold    Leslie Ridge of London, = Louise Smith    Majorie       Dudley Ridge of Brighton, = Winifred Violet Lowden    Leslie
          Eng. b. 1902 d. 1939    m. 1927                         Gentleman. b. 1900          b. 1901 m. 1925           ob. inf.

         Harold Laurence Ridge of Hamilton, = Lois Maud Jackson          Alan Dudley Ridge of Brighton = Irene Geraldine Ames
         Ontairo. b. 1937                    b. 1935 m. 1960             Gentleman. b. 1926             b. 1932 m. 1953

                Carolyn Lesley    Jonathan Kevin Laurence       Wendy Diane Lawson of = Simon Gervase Ridge         Timothy Piers of
                b.1964            b.1971                        Canada. b.1955 m.1973   of London b.1954            Doncaster b.1961

                                                                        Christopher Geoffrey b. 1973
```

IFORD BRANCH

Stephen Ridge of Iford = Jane Alchorne
d. 1664

Stephen Ridge of Westmeston, = Joan Marchant
Yeoman

William Ridge of Iford, = (1) Hannah Packham
Yeoman. b. 1638 d. 1708   (2) Mary Carter

[DIRECT DESCENT]

John Samuel Benjamin Ridge = Sarah Swaine Stephen Hannah Jane Ann Mary Sarah = William Ridge Ann Stephen Mary
               of Iford   of Lewes   ob. inf.   of Lewes   ob. inf. ob. inf. ob. inf.
               Gentleman   m. 1722   Gentleman
               b. 1678 d. 1758

William Ridge of = Elizabeth Ade   Benjamin   Samuel Ridge of = Sarah Sawyers   William   Mary   Sarah = William Ridge
Rottingdean   Iford, Gentleman d. 1800   of Lewes
Gentleman   b. 1723 d. 1772   Gentleman

CHICHESTER BRANCH

Joseph Ridge of = Elizabeth Snashall   Benjamin   Anna   William Ridge = Sarah Ridge   Elizabeth   Mary   Sarah Ridge = Samuel Snashall
Lewes, Surgeon   ob. inf.   of Alicston   of Lewes   d. 1835   of Lewes,
                                                             Gentleman   b. 1758   Gentleman
                                                             b. 1759 d. 1832 m. 1784 d. 1843   d. 1782

Samuel Banjamin Thomas Joseph   Henry Ridge (unmarried)   Anna = Henry Greenhill
                                                  b. 1792 d. 1871

George   William Ridge (unmarried)
d. 1827   of Stoneham
                  Gentleman
                  b. 1787 d. 1848

INDEX

A'Ridge, Aridge (Ridge): 14, 21, 23
Abergavenny (Bergavenny), Lord: 7
Abinger, Baron: 52
Act of Indulgence: 26
Act of Uniformity: 25, 29
Ade: Elizabeth, 24; Richard, 15; Thomas, 9; William, Composition for Knighthood, 23
Age of Reason, The: 30
Alchorne, Jane: 24
Alciston Place: 47
Allington, Manor of: 51
Ames, Irene Geraldine (b. 1932): 61
Arches, Manor of, Framfield: 24
Aridge, Stephen, Composition for knighthood: 23
Artificers, Statute of: 19
Aylwin, John: 22

Baldslow: Hundred of, 2; Richard of, 2
Barnard, Rev. Thomas: 25, 29
Barons, Norman: 4
Bergavenny *see* Abergavenny
Black Death: 5
Boldee Farm, Barcombe: 21
Borough English, Custom of: 9, 13
Botting, Agnes (née Ridge): 12
de Bretagne, John: 2
Bull Lane, Lewes: 30
Burnt House Farm, Fletching: 51, 54
Buttery: 16
Byng, Commodore: 37

Canterbury Cathedral: 36
Carter: Hannah, 24; Mary, 24
Central Registry (1837): 1
Chairman, Ann: 33
de la Chambre: family, 22; Hannah (née Carter), 24; Jane, 24; William, 24
Charles I: 22
Chatham Dock: 36
Cockle, Elizabeth: 33
Comet of 1769: 43
Common Fields: 5, 8
Conventicle Acts: 25
Cook, Miss, of Wisbech: 36
Copyhold Land, Enfranchisement of: 8
Copyhold Tenants: 8
Court Farm, Alciston: 47

Court Leet and Roll: 5, 7, 8
Court Roll, Copy of: 8
Cromwell, Gregory: 14
Customs Rates, Revision of: 19
Custumal of the Manor: 7

Danegeld: 23
Degge, Emily Barnes, 58; Joseph, 56
Dissenters, Independent: 29
Dissenters, Presbyterian: 29
Dissolution of the Monasteries: 9, 13
Ditchling: 26
Dodridge, Rev. Dr: 32
Domesday Book: 14
Drought of 1743-4: 33
Dumbrill, Richard: 15

Ejection of Ministers: 26
Eu, Countess of: 2

Farmhouse, mediaeval: 17
Fealty: 8
Feudal System: 4, 7
Field: Common 5; Open: 5
Floods at Lewes: 42
Franklin: 5
Free Land: 9
Frost, Severe (1739): 42

Gage: family; 47; Sir John, 47
Gentility, Definition of: 22
Gentleman: 7, 28
Goring, Sir Henry: 30
Greenhill, Anna: 53
Gundrada: 13

Hall: 16
Hall House: 16
Harman, James: 21
Harvard University: 29
Harvest Home: 18
Hastings: Matthew of, 2; Rape of, 2
Heriot: 8
Hodgkins, Paradine: 56
Horsfield, Rev. T.W.: 1
Howell, Mary: 23, 24
Hricge (Ridge): 2
Hundred Roll (Sussex): 2
Husbandman: 7, 9

Iford: 13, 20; Constable of, 21; Farm House: 14
Independents: 29, 30
Indulgence, Act of: 26
Industrial Revolution: 17
Inns: Angel, Tunbridge Wells, 35; Bluebell, nr. Maidstone, 36; Bull, Maidstone, 36; Cock, Burton (Boughton), 36; Cock, Dartford, 35; Crown, Sevenoaks, 35; George, Lydd, 37; George, Rye 37; King Henry, Gad's Hill, 36; Maiden Head, Uckfield, 35; Pelican, Hythe, 37; Rose and Crown, Romney, 37; Rose and Crown, Tonbridge, 35; Ship, Dover, 37; Ship, Hastings, 38; Swan, Falmer, 51; Swan, Hastings, 38; White Hart, Sevenoaks Common, 35
Inventory, Post mortem: 15

Jenkin's Ear, War of: 12
Jessop, Martha: 55
Johnston, Mary (née Ridge): 32
Johnston: Rev. Ebenezer, 31, 32, 35, 38: Children of, 38; Journal of, 35 et seq, 40; Marriage of, 32; Ordination of: 31
Journey into Kent, Account of: 35

Kingston, Manor of: 38
Knighthood, Compounding for, 23; Obligations of: 22
Knowle Park: 35

Land: Copyhold, 8; Free, 9
Land Tax: 42, 51, 54
Law of Property Act (1925): 8
Lease, Tenure by: 9
Lewes: Barony of, 7, 45
Lewes: Borough of, 45
Lewes: Borough of, Constables, 45; Officers, 45; 'The Twelve', 45
Lewes: Municipal Borough of (1881), 45; First Mayor, 45
Lewes: Rape of, 13
Lord of the Manor: 4, 7
Lowden, Winifred Violet (b.1901): 60

Maitland: Elizabeth (née Ridge), 38, 39; Robert, 38
Manor Court: 7, 8
Manor: Custumal of the, 7; Lord of the, 4, 7; Steward of the, 7
Manorial System: 4
Marchant, Joan: 26
Mediaeval farmhouse: 16

Memorandoms, Book of: 28, 33, 40, 42
Military Duties: 18
de Militibus, Statute of: 22
Ministers, Ejection of: 25
Monasteries, Dissolution of: 9, 13

Newton, Rev. Edward: 29
Niworde (Iford): 14
Norman Barons: 4
Northease-cum-Iford, Manor of: 5, 9, 12, 27
Norton Down: 12; Farm, 12

Olive, Rev. John: 30
Open Fields: 5, 8
Ote Hall, Wivelsfield: 53
Ovingdean: 12, 20
Owling: 20

Packham: Ann, 29, 45; Hannah, 24; Mary, 24
Paine, Tom: 30
Palmer: Mr, of Ranscombe, 35, 38; Sarah, 50
Pantry: 16
Parish Registers (1537): 1
Parlour: 16
Payment in kind: 9
Peasants' Revolt: 7
Pedigree, Construction of: 1
Pest House, erection of: 45, 46
Poll Tax: 23
Pollington: Agnes, 11; Richard, 11
Post Mortem Inventory: 15
Presbyterians: 29, 30
Priory of St. Pancras: 13, 14

Rape of Hastings: 2
Rape of Lewes: 13
Reason, The Age of: 30
Reeve: 15
Registers, Parish (1537): 1
Registry, Somerset House (1837): 1
Ridge: Adam (ca. 1270): 2
    Agnes (née Pollington)(d.1559), 11, 14
    Alan Dudley (b.1926), 60
    Ann Elizabeth (née Hodgkins) (d.1929), 56, 57, 58
    Benjamin (d.1758), 44
    Benjamin (d.1849), 47, 50
        children of, 50, 52
        death of, 52
        marriage of, 48
        property of, 51
    Charles Henry (d.1948), 58
    Dudley (b.1900), 59, 60
    Emily Barnes (née Degge)(d.1948),

Index

Ridge family: Chichester branch, 24
    Iford branch, 24
    Lewes branch, 24
    Southover branch, 24, 25
    Vault, 33, 38
  George (d.1598), 15
  George Henry (d.1883), 1, 55
    Marriage of, 55
  Harold Lawrence (b.1937), 61
  Henry (d.1871) of Stoneham, 8, 14 53
  Henry (d.1890), 55, 56
    children of, 57
    death of, 58
  Irene Geraldine (née Ames) (b.1932), 61
  Joane (d.1609), 13
  John (d.1710), 17
  John of Iford (d.1612), 11, 13, 14, 18, 19, 20
    children of, 14
  John of Ovingdean (d.1558), 1, 2, 11, 12
    children of, 11
  John of Stoneham (d.1778), 30, 33, 36, 38, 40
    children of, 33
  John of Southover, Constable (1741), 45
    Headborough (1739), 45
  Joseph of Iford, 40
    trustee, 48, 52
  Joseph, Surgeon (d.1816), 46
  Lois Maud (née Jackson)(b.1935), 61
  Mary (ca.1740), 32
  Richard (d.1755), 27, 29, 31
    children of, 29, 30
    Commonplace Book of, 29
  Richard (d.1826), 1, 48, 53
    children of, 52, 54
    disinherited, 48
    legacies to children of, 52
    marriage of, 48
  Sarah (d.1811), 44, 50
  Simon Gervase (b.1954), 61
  Stephen I (d.1638), 14, 15, 21, 26
    children of, 21, 22
    Composition for knighthood, 23
    Constable of Iford (1615), 21
  Stephen II (d.1664), 23
    children of, 23, 24, 25, 26
    second marriage of, 23, 24
  Stephen III (d.1714), 20, 26, 28
    children of, 26
  Stephen of Chailey (d.1736), 26, 27
  Thomas (ca. 1270), 2
  Thomas (d.1736), funeral of, 30
    Headborough (1727), 45
  Thomas of the Cliffe (d.1678), 24, 25, 29,45
  Timothy Piers (b.1961), 61
  William of Alciston (d.1832), 47, 53
    trustee, 48
  William of Lewes (d.1802), 29, 40, 53
    children of, 44, 45, 47, 48
    Constable (1772), 46
    death of, 48
    Headborough (1762), 46
    legacies of, 48, 55
    marriage of, 44
  William of Rottingdean (ca.1729), 9
  William of Stoneham (d.1848), 8, 53
  Winifred Violet (née Lowden), (b.1901), 60
Rochester Cathedral: 36
Rowe: John, 7, 8, 14; Book of, 8, 14, 45
Royal George, the: 36
Royal Liver Friendly Society: 56
Royal London Friendly Soceity: 58; Arms of, 57; Foundation of, 56

St. Anne's House, Lewes, 50, 51
  Edmundsbury: Priory of, 7
  Mary's Lane, Lewes: 25
  Michael's Church, Lewes: 30
    Ridge family vault: 31
  Pancras: Priory of, 13, 14
  Wulfran: 11
Scarlett, James: 52
Service: Commutation of, 5: Tenure by, 4
Silk Mill, Sevenoaks: 35
Skinner, James of London: 51
Smugglers: 37
Smuggling: 19
Snashall: Samuel, 32, 40, 53
  Trustee, 48

Snashall, Sarah, (née Ridge): 53
Somerset House Registry (1837): 1
Southover: 13
Star, Rev. Comfort: 29
Statute of Artificers: 19
Stoneham Farm, Upper: 27, 30
Surfdom: 7
Surnames, derivation of: 2
Swan Inn, Falmer: 51

Tenants, Copyhold: 8
Tenure by Lease: 9
Tilbury Fort: 35
Tully Wells, Hamsey: 30
Turner: Ann of Fletching, 48; Richard (ca.1741), 45
Twelve, The: 45

Uniformity, Act of: 25, 29
Upper Stoneham Farm: 27, 29, 30

Villein: 4
Vynall, John, of Kingston: 21

de Warenne, Earl: 7, 13, 14
Weller, Cruttenden: 32, 33, 45
Westgate Meeting House, Lewes: 29-31, 38, 40, 53
Westmeston: 26
Widow's Bench, Right of: 9
William the Conqueror: 4, 7, 13
Withdean Cayliffe, Manor of: 12
Woodbrookes Farm: 20, 26, 30, 47, 50, 52; Law Suit, 27
Wool, Export duties on: 19
Work Days: 5, 7

Yeoman: 5, 7, 9; The first, 13 Literacy of the, 18
Yeoman's family: 17; way of life, 17